Burt Franklin Bibliography & Reference Series #93

THE DEVELOPMENT OF
FREEDOM OF THE PRESS
IN MASSACHUSETTS

THE DEVELOPMENT OF FREEDOM OF THE PRESS IN MASSACHUSETTS

BY

CLYDE AUGUSTUS DUNIWAY

BURT FRANKLIN
New York, N.Y.

Published by BURT FRANKLIN
235 East 44th St., New York 10017
Originally Published: New York 1906
Reprinted: 1969
Printed in the U.S.A. on long-life paper.

Library of Congress Catalog Card No.: 68-58770
Burt Franklin: Bibliography & Reference Series #93

PREFACE.

THIS monograph is the result of an extended revision of a thesis for the degree of Doctor of Philosophy in Political Science, which was accepted by Harvard University in 1897. That thesis, entitled " The History of Restrictions upon the Freedom of the Press in Massachusetts," was honored in the same year by the award of the Toppan prize.

Some fourteen years ago the author formed the plan of writing a comprehensive history of the right of freedom of discussion in the United States. As a first step, an investigation of restrictions upon the freedom of the press in British-American colonies was undertaken. Research in all printed materials for historical study of the period yielding results of unexpected paucity, it became evident that no satisfactory treatment of the topic was possible without examination of unpublished manuscript archives in England and in each of the colonies within the scope of the inquiry. The magnitude of the task led to a decision to limit the investigation to Massachusetts. In that narrower field it seemed possible to treat every aspect of the subject with sufficient fulness to give a true picture of historic development; but even here the loss of contemporary records in a few instances has prevented the solution of certain problems. In the main, however, the results set forth in the following pages should explain the significant features of the rise of a free press in Massachusetts.

The point of view maintained throughout has required that treatment of questions and influences external to Massachusetts should be kept strictly subordinate to the main topic. The effects of British precedents and of imperial regulations in the colonial period have been duly considered, and incidental allusions to parallel developments in other states have been introduced in the footnotes; but there has been no attempt at any adequate discussion of the wider relations of the general subject, or of events which have not apparently influenced the status of the press in Massachusetts.

The thanks of the author are due to many persons for courtesies extended in the prosecution of this work. Especial mention should be made of the late Professor Moses Coit Tyler, under whose advice the investigation was first carried on at Cornell University, and of Professor Edward Channing, under whose guidance the detailed research was continued at Harvard University. Professor Albert Bushnell Hart of Harvard University, Mr. A. C. Goodell, editor of the Massachusetts "Acts and Resolves," Mr. E. M. Barton of the American Antiquarian Society, Mr. John Noble, clerk of the Supreme Court of Judicature of Suffolk County (with his obliging assistants), and the helpful clerks in the archives department of the office of the secretary of the commonwealth have conferred special favors upon the author. Miss A. F. Rowe of Cambridge has carefully verified all references to and quotations from manuscript sources. My wife has given material assistance in literary revision and in proof-reading and indexing.

CLYDE AUGUSTUS DUNIWAY.

STANFORD UNIVERSITY,
December 1, 1905.

CONTENTS.

CHAPTER I.

CONTROL OF THE PRESS IN ENGLAND TO 1603.

CHAPTER II.

RESTRICTION OF DISCUSSION IN ENGLAND AND MASSACHUSETTS, 1603–1640.

CHAPTER III.

SUPERVISION OF THE PRESS, 1638–1662.

CHAPTER IV.

RESTRICTIVE CENSORSHIP, 1662–1685.

CHAPTER V.

LAX ENFORCEMENT OF CENSORSHIP, 1686–1716.

CHAPTER VI.

LAST EFFORTS TO MAINTAIN CENSORSHIP, 1716–1723.

CHAPTER VII.

LIMITED FREEDOM OF THE PRESS, 1723-1763.

CHAPTER VIII.

REVOLUTIONARY FREEDOM AND CONSTITUTIONAL GUARANTEES, 1763-1789.

CHAPTER IX.

REACTIONARY TENDENCIES, 1789–1812, AND MODI-
FICATION OF THE LAW OF LIBEL, 1807–1827.

APPENDIXES.

THE DEVELOPMENT OF THE FREEDOM OF THE PRESS.

---◆---

CHAPTER I.

CONTROL OF THE PRESS IN ENGLAND, TO 1603.

SINCE the invention of printing in Europe, the world has witnessed a gradual but imperfect substitution of public discussion through the press for the difficult circulation of manuscripts and the narrowly restricted agency of public meetings and mere public speech. Although the diffusion of printed matter has not taken, and can never entirely take, the place of personal association and the spoken word in public and private assemblies, nevertheless the marvellous utility of the press as an instrument of public discussion has given it a place of transcendent importance in the determination of political and social questions.[1] That the evolution of thought and of institutions for more than four centuries has been conditioned by the influence of the press, is a historical truism.

[1] Some well-known eulogies on the power of the press are those by Milton, *Areopagitica;* Erskine, argument in Rex *v.* Paine, Howell, *State Trials,* xxii. 410; Mackintosh, in Rex *v.* Peltier, *Ibid.* xxviii. 563; Curran, in Rex *v.* Rowan, *Ibid.* xxii. 1066; Junius, *Letters,* Preface; Camden, in Cobbett, *Parliamentary History,* xxix. 731; Fox, *Ibid.* 553; Macaulay, *England,* ch. x; May, *Constitutional History,* ch. ix; Lecky, *England,* iii. 284 ff. Present-day development of the printing business may be seen in the great publishers' catalogues and in the "newspaper annuals" of advertising agencies. See also S. N. D. North's special report on "The Newspaper and Periodical Press," in United States *Tenth Census,* viii.

The development of a democratic polity in the modern world has been accompanied by a readjustment of the status of the right of freedom of discussion, — a right comprehending freedom of speech, freedom of assembly, and freedom of the press.[1]   From the standpoint of rulers by divine right, there could be no right of freedom of discussion, but merely some degree of privilege allowed or withheld by themselves for reasons of state.   From the standpoint of members of a constituent electorate, the enjoyment of this right in its various forms has been necessary for the exercise of their political functions; yet representative legislative bodies have not merely maintained against executive interference the defensive "privilege" of freedom of debate, but have also long upheld, even against their constituents, the paradoxical "privilege" of keeping their proceedings exempt from public comment and from report.   These two elements in government, the monarchical and the representative, have usually agreed in denying to non-enfranchised classes the right of freedom of discussion.   Even when a broad basis of popular representation has been established, persistence of governmental control has often subjected minorities to the tyranny of majorities.   For, although a free society may accord a generous recognition to freedom of discussion, the community must protect itself against abuse of all individual rights; and it is precisely here — in the regulation of acts which may be obnoxious to common right and justice — that the problem of freedom of discussion presents itself for solution.   In politics as well as in religion, obedience to the first law of any institution — that is, to self-preserva-

---

[1] Some suitable phrase must be used to express the larger idea which embraces freedom of the press, freedom of speech, and freedom of assembly. The expression "freedom of discussion" commends itself as conveying that idea. Lieber (*Civil Liberty*, 87) uses the rather antiquated phrase, "freedom of communion." In English public constitutional practice, freedom of the press has become one of the "liberties of the subject."

tion — has seemed to require coercive maintenance of orthodox standards of faith and practice.[1]

The significance of this issue in the English-speaking world since the end of the fifteenth century is illustrated most clearly by prolonged contests over the status of the press. Efforts to secure freedom of speech and freedom of assembly as primary rights of the subject continued to be of great importance; but all forms of agitation and propaganda sought expression through the press, and became identified with the advocacy of relaxation of restrictions upon its freedom.

The establishment of a printing-press in Westminster by William Caxton in 1476–77 was the result of special royal encouragement and grant of privileges,[2] and the business activity of Caxton himself and of his fellow-craftsmen in sundry towns of England was dependent upon the continued favor of sovereigns, which was secured by judicious abstinence from printing controversial or heterodox works.[3] While the industry was in its infancy and there

---

[1] For summary accounts of limitations upon freedom of discussion before the invention of printing, see encyclopedic articles on "Index Librorum Prohibitorum" and "Bibliography." Similarly, for general outline treatments of national press restrictions, see articles on "Press Laws"; and see also Putnam, *Books and their Makers*, ii. *passim*. The best brief secondary account of the history of English press restrictions is by Paterson, *Liberty of the Press, Speech, and Public Worship*, a book marred by sundry mistakes of fact, which are, however, relatively unimportant and detract little from its value. See also Hunt, *Fourth Estate;* Andrews, *British Journalism;* Grant, *The Newspaper Press;* Bourne, *English Newspapers;* Lecky, Hume, May, Macaulay, *passim:* all have more or less to say upon the topic. The agency of Christian theologians in repressing freedom of scientific discussion is fully set forth in Andrew D. White's *Warfare of Science with Theology.*

[2] Blades, *Caxton*, i. ch. vi. Caxton enjoyed the patronage of Edward IV, Richard III, and Henry VII.

[3] See lists of works printed by Caxton and other early English printers. The English people, as well as the world in general, had long been familiar with punishment of politico-theological heresy. See, for example, 5 Richard II, st. 2, c. 5; 2 Henry IV, c. 15; 2 Henry V, st. 1, c. 7.

were few books and few printers within the realm, special
privileges were extended even to aliens who might import
books, or who might come into England as booksellers or
as "scriveners, alluminors, readers or printers";[1] but
when products of the press multiplied in considerable
quantities, closer supervision of its issues became necessary.[2] Regulations for the "mystery" limited the numbers of printers and their apprentices, and royal patents
were issued creating monopolies in the printing trade.[3]
Soon proclamations by bishops and by the king prohibited
the importation, printing, and circulation of various categories of books, especially English translations of the New
Testament.[4] In December, 1534, Henry VIII issued a
severe and detailed measure, "The King's Proclamation
for Seditious Books," commanding in part that no one
should print any English book without a license either
from the Privy Council or from other persons appointed
by the king as licensers.[5] The king's demands for the
success of his reformation of the national church then led

[1] 1 Richard III, c. 19. Duff (*Early Printed Books*, chs. vii–x) discusses
the beginnings and the spread of printing in various parts of England.

[2] The act of 1483, favoring alien printers, was repealed in 1533 by 25 Henry
VIII, c. 15. The reasons for the repeal as set forth in the act are as follows :
"Since the making of the said provision many of this realm, being the
king's natural subjects, have given themselves so diligently to learn and
exercise the said craft of printing that at this day there be within this
realm a great number, cunning and expert in the said science or craft of
printing as able to exercise the said craft in all points as any stranger in any
other realm or country."

[3] See Cobbett, *Parliamentary History*, xvii. 958, 993 (arguments of Sir
John Dalrymple and Lord Camden in the case of Beckett *v.* Denison). A
"king's printer," Richard Pynson, was appointed early in the reign of
Henry VIII. See *Letters and Papers, Foreign and Domestic, Henry VIII*,
i. 154.

[4] Strype, *Cranmer*, 81–82; Arber, *Transcript of Registers of the Company
of Stationers*, v. p. li.

[5] Strype, *Cranmer*, 685–691 ; also Strype, *Memorials*, i. pt. i. 341, pt. ii.
228–230.

to statutes and royal injunctions and proclamations which forbade the use of the press in the maintenance of the new heresies.[1] In 1542–43 Parliament was induced to give sweeping statutory sanction to the absolute authority of the crown to regulate the press and every other means of public discussion;[2] and the strife of religious parties

[1] See the Six Articles Act, 31 Henry VIII, c. 14. Injunctions of 1539 are analyzed in Strype, *Memorials*, i. pt. i. 530–532. On the proclamation for " an Uniformity in Religion," see *Ibid.* 547 ; and for the inquiry after heretical books at Oxford in 1540, *Ibid.* 565, 569–570.

[2] 34 & 35 Henry VIII, c. 1. The provisions of this " Act for the Advancement of true Religion and for the Abolishment of the Contrary " are as follows : " Recourse must be had to the catholick and apostolick church for the decision of controversies ; and therefore all books of the Old and New Testament in *English*, being of *Tindal's* false translation, or comprising any matter of christian religion, articles of the faith, or holy scripture, contrary to the doctrine set forth sithence *Anno Dom.* 1540, or to be set forth by the King, shall be abolished. No printer or bookseller shall utter any of the aforesaid books. No persons shall play in interlude, sing or rhime, contrary to the said doctrine. No person shall retain any *English* books or writings concerning matter against the holy and blessed sacrament of the altar, or for the maintenance of anabaptists, or other books abolished by the King's proclamation. There shall be no annotations or preambles in Bibles or New Testaments in *English*. The Bible shall not be read in *English* in any church. No women or artificers, prentices, journeymen, servingmen of the degree of yeomen or under, husbandmen, nor labourers, shall read the New Testament in *English*. Nothing shall be taught or maintained contrary to the King's instructions. And if any spiritual person preach, teach, or maintain any thing contrary to the King's instructions or determinations, made or to be made, and shall be thereof convict, he shall for his first offence recant, for his second abjure and bear a fagot, and for his third shall be adjudged an heretick, and be burned and lose all his goods and chattels." The sweeping character of the statute is marked by the clauses, " or to be set forth by the King," " or other books abolished by the King's proclamation," " nothing shall be taught or maintained contrary to the King's instructions," " contrary to the King's instructions or determinations, made or to be made." In this connection, see also act of 31 Henry VIII, c. 8, recognizing proclamations by king and council as having the force of law. The fact that this act was repealed by 1 Edward VI, c. 12, did not alter in practice the constitutional status of proclamations. See Dicey, *Privy Council*, 105–109 ; Reeves, *History of English Law*, v. 471 ; Burn, *The Star Chamber, passim ;* Medley, *Constitutional History*, 85–87 ; Gardiner, *Charles I*, i. 161.

perpetuated this principle, and practice in accordance with it, throughout the successive reigns of the Tudors. The government of Edward VI, no less than the reactionary rule of Mary and Philip, sought to enforce penalties against all advocacy of dissent.[1] In 1556 the definite incorporation of an ancient fellowship as the Stationers' Company established an organization designed to provide more adequate supervision and regulation of the press;[2] and numerous supplementary proclamations, injunctions, and decrees in the Star Chamber continued to be utilized to the same purpose.[3] Queen Elizabeth issued injunctions in the first year of her reign, prescribing that no manner of book or paper in any language should be printed without her Majesty's express license, or the license of six of the Privy Council or of the archbishops, the bishops, the archdeacons, or the chancellors of the universities; and that no pamphlets, plays, or ballads should be printed

---

[1] The Privy Council of Edward VI enforced the requirement of licenses. On August 13, 1549, it passed an order "that from henceforth no printer should print, or put to vent, any English book but such as should first be examined by Mr. Secretary Peter, Mr. Secretary Smith, and Mr. Cecil, or the one of them, and allowed by the same" (*Acts of Privy Council,* 1547–1550, pp. 311–312). An instance of enforcement is given in Strype, *Cranmer,* 901–902. Certain licenses and monopoly privileges to print are noted in Strype, *Memorials,* ii. pt. i. 552, and pt. ii. 40, 114–115, 240. On August 18, 1553, Mary issued a proclamation prohibiting all printing without special license : see Arber, *Transcript,* v. p. xl ; Fox, *Acts and Monuments,* vi. 390–391. Also see Philip and Mary's proclamation of June 13, 1555, in Arber, *Transcript,* i. 52 ; Strype, *Memorials,* iii. pt. i. 417–418.

[2] Arber, *Transcript,* i. p. xxviii, v. p. xxxix. The purpose to establish the company as a means of control for the press is clearly expressed in the charter. The master printers included in the corporation got commercial advantages from their monopolistic privileges. They worked in coöperation with ecclesiastical authorities to supervise the press.

[3] There were many special patents besides the charter of the Company of Stationers (see Arber, *Transcript,* i. 111, 114–116, 144, 246–248, ii. 60–64, 746–747, 817–819, 886). A most interesting and graphic account of the state of the printing business is contained in Christopher Barker's report, in December, 1582, on the patents from 1558 to 1582 (*Ibid.* i. 114).

without the license of three of the ecclesiastical commissioners in London. The only exceptions under these
sweeping prohibitions were the works of classical authors,
and those that had heretofore been commonly used in
schools and universities.[1]

The difficulties of enforcing this system of monopoly
limitation and censorship led, in 1566, to the first Star
Chamber ordinance for the regulation of printing,[2] which
in turn had to be supplemented, in 1586, by the detailed
measures of the second Star Chamber ordinance on the
subject. This provided, under severe penalties, (1) that
every printer must register an account of his press and
materials with the master and wardens of the Company of
Stationers; (2) that no presses would be allowed outside
of the city of London, except one each in the universities
of Cambridge and Oxford, and all were to be in places
subject to free inspection by the wardens of the Company
of Stationers; (3) that the archbishop of Canterbury, the
bishop of London, and the high commissioners in causes
ecclesiastical, should regulate the number of presses and
printers; (4) that, with certain privileged exceptions,
nothing should be printed without a license from the archbishop of Canterbury and the bishop of London, or from
one of them; (5) that the wardens of the Company of
Stationers should be the authorized agents to enforce these
regulations, bringing offenders before the high commissioners in causes ecclesiastical for examination and punishment; (6) that the number of printers' apprentices should
be strictly limited.[3]

All these regulations, affording ample scope for the

---

[1] Arber, *Transcript*, i. xxxviii; Prothero, *Statutes*, 188–189.

[2] Arber, *Transcript*, i. 322; Strype, *Parker*, i. 442–443; Neal, *Puritans*,
i. 250–251; Prothero, *Statutes*, 168–169. The ordinance was passed upon
recommendation of the ecclesiastical commissioners.

[3] Strype, *Whitgift*, i. 422–425; Prothero, *Statutes*, 169–172; Arber,
Transcript, ii. 807–812.

activities of persecuting churchmen and courtiers, had not wholly prevented bold and clandestine circulation of proscribed printed matter by religious and political agitators.[1] Nevertheless, throughout the whole period from the introduction of printing until the beginnings of English colonization, the crown lawfully exercised sovereign control over the press, as over every other agency of public discussion;[2] and, as the great significance of the problem of adjustment between claims of authority and freedom of discussion was barely emerging in the social consciousness of the English people by the end of the sixteenth century, the principle of governmental regulation of the press would easily pass, by a natural inheritance, into typical colonial institutions.

[1] On Puritan libels under Elizabeth, see Hallam, *Constitutional History*, i. 207–209. The cases of Stubbs and Page, Barrow and Greenwood, Penry, Udall, and Throckmorton are well known. Documents showing seizures of books are given by Arber, *Transcript*, i. 393–394, 492, ii. 38–40, iii. 677–678. See also Strype, *Grindal*, 516–519, and *Aylmer*, 45.

[2] The House of Commons showed some disposition to pass special statutes on the subject in 1550 and 1566 (see *Commons Journals*, i. 14, 15, 77). In 1581, also, it condemned and punished one of its members, Mr. Arthur Hall, for the publication of a book deemed derogatory to Parliament (*Ibid.* 122, 124, 125, 126, 127, 136).

CHAPTER II.

RESTRICTION OF DISCUSSION IN ENGLAND AND MASSACHUSETTS, 1603–1640.

THE spirit of the government of James I, so far as it depended upon the king himself, was well expressed in a sentence of his speech in the Star Chamber on June 20, 1616. "It is atheism and blasphemy," said he, "to dispute what God can do: good Christians content themselves with his will revealed in his word, so it is presumption and high contempt in a subject to dispute what a king can do, or say that a king cannot do this or that; but rest in that which is the king's revealed will in his law."[1]

Here, then, was a royal denial of the right of freedom of discussion in England, in anything that concerned the sovereign or that he chose to consider as his interest. The only semblance of a right of freedom of speech depended upon a vague, varying, and narrowly limited "privilege of Parliament" to enjoy freedom of debate, a privilege repeatedly denied by the crown and often infringed by the intolerance of Parliament itself.[2] Freedom of assembly was an unrecognized right, any assembly which the

[1] Prothero, *Statutes*, 400. See also an earlier statement of the same principle in a speech before Parliament on March 21, 1610: "That as to dispute what God may do is blasphemy . . . so is it sedition in subjects to dispute what a king may do in the height of his power" (*Ibid.* 294). James I held himself to be "above the law by his absolute power," a doctrine to which Dr. Cowell assented and for which he was attacked by Parliament (*Ibid.* 409–411).

[2] See the instructive selections from the documents printed in Prothero, *Statutes*, 117–126, 296–298.

9

executive power chose to forbid was deemed unlawful,[1] and the statutes abounded in prohibitions of unauthorized meetings. Nor could freedom of the press be said to exist while the crown continued to maintain the strict system of surveillance which had been built up in preceding reigns.

Since 1559 the court of High Commission had supplemented the work of the court of Star Chamber, by exercising a general authority to inquire into and punish all heresies and seditions.[2] In 1613 James I added to the powers of the High Commission specific jurisdiction over "all other books, pamphlets and portraitures offensive to the state or set forth without sufficient and lawful authority in that behalf . . . and also all persons which shall offend against any decree heretofore made by the high court of Star-Chamber . . . or hereafter to be there made touching the reformation of divers disorders in the printing and uttering of books." [3]   Not even these great powers satisfied the high-prerogative and high-church parties in their efforts to suppress publications favoring their adversaries.[4] Laud in particular, both while he was bishop of London

---

[1] The power was exercised by the crown through the issue of proclamations, which were very common under the Tudors and Stuarts. See Arber, *Transcript*, i. 52, 92, 452.

[2] "Seditious books" are specially mentioned in the commissions (Prothero, *Statutes*, 227–228). It is worthy of note that in 1604 a bill to reform abuses in importing, printing, buying, and selling "seditious, Popish, vain and lascivious Books," passed the Lords, was considered by the Commons for some time, and then, as the record quaintly says, was "dashed, without One Yea.— Weariness and Want of Time" (*Lords Journals*, ii. 308 ; *Commons Journals*, i. 229, 233, 244, 245, 249, 252). See also 3 James I, c. 5, §§ 25, 26, directed against all popish books, — another parliamentary sanction of press regulation.

[3] Prothero, *Statutes*, 427–428.

[4] The enforcement of these regulations and penalties varied with the character and the policy of the head of the High Commission. Arber (*Transcript*, iii. pp. 13–14) concludes that censorship was mild under Parker and Grindal (1559–1583), rigid under Whitgift and Bancroft (1583–1610), mild again under Abbot (1611–1633), and very severe under Laud (1633–1645).

and after he became archbishop of Canterbury, was most persistent in preventing and punishing unauthorized printing. Finding by experience that previous orders were somewhat defective,[1] he secured the promulgation of the Star Chamber decree of 1637, which provided a complete scheme of control in the following regulations: —

I. No one should, anywhere in the king's dominions, print, bind, import, or sell anything seditious, schismatical, or offensive, to the scandal of religion or the church or the government, or of governors of the church or state, or of the commonwealth, or of any corporation, or of a particular person or persons.[2]

II. Nothing might be printed unless first lawfully licensed and entered in the register's book of the Company of Stationers.

III. Common law books must be licensed by the lord chief justices and the lord chief baron ; histories and books relating to state affairs by the secretaries of state ; books of heraldry and the like by the earl marshal ; all other books — of divinity, physic, philosophy, poetry, or anything else — by the lord archbishop of Canterbury, or the bishop of London, or the chancellors or vice-chancellors of the universities, provided that the universities did not meddle with books of common law or matters of state, but licensed only books to be printed at the universities.

IV. Every licenser must have two written and complete copies of the several books licensed by him, on which he must certify that there was nothing in them " contrary to Christian Faith, and the Doctrine and Discipline of the Church of England, nor against the State or Government,

---

[1] Rushworth (*Collections*, ii. 450) explains that Laud wished to prevent the reprinting of books of divinity which had been formerly licensed but were objectionable to him.

[2] This provision gave authority for the punishment of unlawful publications even in the colonies, — a threat, however ineffective, against the Puritans.

nor contrary to good life, or good manners"; and this license or approbation must be printed at the beginning of the book licensed.

V. A true catalogue of all imported books must be furnished the lord archbishop of Canterbury or the lord bishop of London before the said books were offered for sale.

VI. All packages of imported books must, on arrival, be examined by one of the chaplains of the lord archbishop of Canterbury or the lord bishop of London, together with the master and wardens of the Company of Stationers, or one of them; and if prohibited books should be found, they were to be seized and the offenders punished.

VII. Letters patent for the sole right to print, and copyrights, must be respected.

VIII. All printed matter must bear the names of author, printer, and publisher.

IX. The "trade marks" of the Company of Stationers and others must not be counterfeited.

X. No person should deal in books who had not been for seven years an apprentice to a bookseller, a printer, or a bookbinder.

XI. For the encouragement of honest home printers, no books printed in English should be imported.

XII. No foreigner should engage in the book trade except through an agent who was a free stationer of London.

XIII. No person should set up any press or printing-house, or let any place for a printing-house, without notice to the master and wardens of the Company of Stationers.

XIV. No person should make or import any press or type without notifying the said master and wardens for whom these things were made or imported.

XV. Only twenty master printers (here enumerated by name) should be allowed to use presses, vacancies in the number to be filled by the lord archbishop of Canterbury and the lord bishop of London, and six other high commissioners appointed by them.

XVI. Every person allowed to use a press must give sureties in the sum of three hundred pounds to print none but books lawfully licensed.

XVII. No "allowed printer" should keep more than two presses, unless he had been master or upper warden of his company, when he might have three. The lord archbishop of Canterbury or the lord bishop of London was to have full power for the suppressing of supernumerary presses.

XVIII. No book heretofore licensed should be reprinted without being reviewed and getting a new license.

XIX. Every master printer who was or had been master or upper warden of his company might have not more than three apprentices at one time, every master printer of the livery of his company not more than two; and every master printer of the yeomanry of his company not more than one.

XX. The master and wardens of the Company of Stationers should take special care to provide with employment all journeymen printers who were honest, of good behavior, and able in their trade.

XXI. Neglect to provide work for journeymen, and refusal of journeymen to work when required, should both be punished.

XXII. The printers of the universities might take what apprentices they wished, provided they continued to employ all their own journeymen.

XXIII. No master printer should employ in his business any but freemen or "apprentices to the trade or mystery of printing."

XXIV. All unallowed printers should be set in the pillory, whipped through the city of London, and suffer other punishment optional with the court of High Commission.

XXV. The master and wardens of the Company of Stationers, with appointed assistants, should have power to search any house or shop at any time, to view what was being printed, and to seize unlicensed books and offenders against the law.

XXVI. The said searchers should seize suspected books and bring them to the lord archbishop of Canterbury or the lord bishop of London, who were to do with them as they saw fit.

XXVII. The number of type-founders should be limited to four (here named), vacancies to be filled by the lord archbishop of Canterbury or the lord bishop of London and six other high commissioners.

XXVIII. No master founder should keep above two apprentices.

XXIX. All journeymen founders should be employed by the master founders, and all idle journeymen should be compelled to work in the same manner as the journeymen printers.

XXX. No master founder should employ in his business any person (except one boy) who was not a freeman or an apprentice to the trade of founding letters.

XXXI. All persons convicted of any of these many offences must, on discharge, be bound in good sureties never to transgress in a like way again; " seditious schismaticall books " were to be burnt, and other forfeitures to be disposed of as the High Commission should direct "alwaies providing that one moitie be to the King."

XXXII. No books should be imported except at the port of London.

XXXIII. One copy of every printed book must be sent to the University of Oxford, for the use of the public library there.[1]

---

[1] Arber, *English Reprints: Areopagitica*, 7–23; Arber, *Transcript*, iv. 528–536.

The failure of even these elaborate measures to prevent "the printing, importing and dispersing of popish and seditious books and pamphlets and seditious puritanical books and pamphlets . . . grown so common and practised so licentiously, both to the traducing of religion and the state," was virtually acknowledged in special proclamations, issued to stimulate officers to greater watchfulness and to warn offenders that violations of the orders would be punished most severely.[1] Nevertheless, the complaisant officials of the established church and of the prerogative courts, by their activity in enforcing royal decrees, made any attempted evasion exceedingly dangerous and often impossible.[2] If anything was lacking to complete the system of denial of freedom of the press, it was supplied by Parliament in special orders against authors or printers who published anything objectionable to the majority in either house.[3]

Such conditions bore hard upon all minority parties, but with especial severity upon Catholics, Puritans, and Separatists. The Protestant founders of Plymouth Colony and Massachusetts Bay had lived under a régime of persecution and proscription for their dissent from the established order in religion and in politics; yet their sufferings had not led them to plead for a generous and real freedom of discussion, but merely for a toleration of their peculiar tenets. They had, indeed, complained of the undue exaltation of the crown's share in the law-making power as exerted through the Council and the Star Chamber, and they made a grievance of partisan administration of decrees

[1] Prothero, *Statutes*, 394-396 ; Rymer, *Fœdera*, xvii. 522, 616, xviii. 1024–1025, xix. 26, xx. 144–145, 290–293, 346–347, 402–403 ; Rushworth, *Collections*, i. 635, ii. 38, 40, 43, 402, 410–411, 830.

[2] The famous cases of Prynne, Bastwick, and Burton, in 1637, illustrate the dangers of publication "without license first obtained." See Rushworth, *Collections*, ii. 220–241, 380–385.

[3] *Commons Journals*, i. 230, 244, 882, 920–921.

against liberties of the subject;[1] but when Selden spoke in Parliament, in 1628, against the Star Chamber decrees for the control of the press, it was only to demand that there might be a law made on the subject.[2] Not the fact of censorship, but the methods of licensing officers in favor of "popish" doctrines, roused the Puritan party to assail the existing press regulations.[3]

Following, therefore, the ideas prevalent in England at the time, the people who undertook the settlement of Massachusetts did not conceive that there was any legal right of freedom of discussion. That they should stamp out heresy in the church and sedition in the state was a matter of plain necessity, a common-sense regulation for the preservation of public order and for the furtherance of the great purpose that had brought them to New England. Any relaxation of their control would have seemed a surrender of liberty to licentiousness. They kept control of the press as an essential part of their policy to maintain pure religious doctrine and worship, to guard public morality, to preserve a wholesome respect for the authority of magistrates and elders, to defend their charter rights, to give security against the ever dreaded injury from the spread of dangerous ideas.

Before the introduction of a printing-press into Massachusetts, the magistrates had to deal with many cases of "contentious" and "disorderly" expressions of opinion. Even the generous-minded Bradford and his associates in

---

[1] For example, in 1623 and again in 1624, the House of Commons adopted as a grievance the complaint of Mr. Raynscrofte "against printing or selling of Popish books; whereof [he] hath a catalogue of seven or eight score printed within these two years" (*Commons Journals*, i. 709, 712, 796). For a petition presented to the House of Commons in 1628 by printers and book-sellers of London, complaining of restraints on "books written against Popery and Arminianism," see Rushworth, *Collections*, i. 655.

[2] Cobbett, *Parliamentary History*, ii. 463.

[3] See Gardiner, *Constitutional Documents*, 13-16, 69.

Plymouth Colony found it necessary to check religious dissent and seditious practices in their midst. To be sure, they always used somewhat milder methods, executed laws less rigorously, and had fewer cases involving regulation of opinions than troubled the peace of Massachusetts Bay Colony. Yet their policy in these matters was similar to that of their more populous neighbor; and their lack of press laws and the absence of libel prosecutions are fully accounted for by the fact that Plymouth Colony had no printing-press while it existed as a government separate from Massachusetts Bay.[1]

In Massachusetts, Governor Endicott promptly and zealously executed the instructions which he had received to permit no obnoxious persons to remain in his jurisdiction. When, for example, John and Samuel Browne ventured to dissent from the ecclesiastical arrangements made in Salem in 1629, he sternly expelled them from the colony. Their complaints in England against Endicott's high-handed procedure gave the company there so much annoyance for fear that the government would seize the occasion as a pretext for destroying the refuge of these overbold dissenters, that it addressed mild reproofs to the governor, approving the general policy of excluding intruders, but urging the advisability of more discretion and moderation in such cases. The incident served to make one of a long succession of precedents for the regulation of opinions in the colony.[2]

The story of the experiences of Roger Williams in Massachusetts has often been told, because his case is a conspicuous example of the suffering that sprang from the persecuting spirit of American Puritans, and because he is

[1] See Bradford, *Plymouth*, 171–196; see also a law of June 7, 1659, *Plymouth Records*, xi. 121.

[2] *Massachusetts Records*, i. 51–54, 69, 407–409; Palfrey, *New England*, i. 298–299, quoting Morton's *Memorial;* Barry, *Massachusetts*, i. 172.

c

justly revered as one of the great founders of American religious freedom. Independent in thought, disputatious in discourse, aggressive in action, his character made him a storm centre at a time when toleration of free discussion was unthinkable. The only haven of peace for him would have been a community in which he could be the master spirit; and a trial of strength proved that he was not to be allowed to play that rôle in Massachusetts. His first public acts were ominous of trouble, for he refused to officiate in the Boston church because it was an "unseparated" congregation.[1] He developed subversive views as to the validity of the title of the New Plymouth colonists to the land on which they were settled, believing that they could have no good title by the king's patent, or in any other way except by purchase from the Indians; and he embodied his opinions in a treatise which he presented to the Governor and Council of New Plymouth. Governor Winthrop obtained a copy of the treatise, and laid it before the assistants of Massachusetts Bay, who called the author to account. Williams wrote a submissive letter, professing that he had written only for the private satisfaction of the rulers of New Plymouth, and offering his book, or any part of it, to be burned. His penitence led to further consideration of the offensive passages, and "upon his retraction, etc., or taking an oath of allegiance to the king, etc.," they were passed over.[2]

The experiences of 1633 had not taught Roger Williams to walk the straight and narrow path of peace in Massachusetts. He engaged in a controversy over the wearing of veils by women in church. He believed with Endicott that the cross in the English flag was idolatrous

[1] Winthrop, *New England* (Savage ed.), i. 63.

[2] *Ibid.* i. 145–147 (entries of December 27, 1633, and January 24, 1633–34); Bradford, *Plymouth*, 310–311; Barry, *Massachusetts*, i. 236–238.

and should be taken out. He was obnoxiously active as a leader of contentious factions in Salem. He was complained of for breaking his promise by teaching publicly against the king's patent, for calling the churches of England anti-Christian, and for declaring that it was sinful in magistrates to tender oaths to the unregenerate. In July, 1635, he was examined by the General Court, which evidently disapproved of his views, but gave him and his church at Salem time to reconsider the things objected against him. Meanwhile, Salem applied for a grant of land, which the magistrates refused because the town had chosen Williams teacher in the church, "while he stood under question of authority." Williams retaliated by inducing the Salem church to send circular letters to the other churches of Massachusetts Bay, urging them to rebuke the oppression of the magistrates. In this political movement he was assisted by John Endicott and the other Salem leaders, whose contumacious course soon met with sharp reproof. Punishment in varying degrees fell upon the other members of this opposition party ; while Williams brought upon himself the sentence of banishment, and had to flee into the wilderness to avoid deportation to England. Such was the penalty for outspoken and persistent freedom in differing from the majority of the magistrates and ministers.[1]

Soon after the case of Roger Williams events occurred of special significance as showing the status of any sup-

---

[1] *Massachusetts Records*, i. 160–161 ; Winthrop, *New England*, i. 195, 204; Palfrey, *New England*, i. 406–421 ; Barry, *Massachusetts*, i. 238–244. In March, 1635, Israel Stoughton, one of the deputies, incurred the censure of the General Court because he had written a "book" maintaining that assistants were not magistrates and that the governor was not entitled to a "negative voice." The record thus explains the matter : "Whereas Mr Israell Stoughton hath written a certaine booke wch hath occasoned much trouble & offence to the Court, the sd Mr Stoughton did desire of the Court that the sd booke might forthwith be burnt, as being weake and offensive."

posed right of free discussion. In 1637 the brilliant
Anne Hutchinson became the cause of the most serious
disturbance which the colony of Massachusetts Bay had
yet passed through, a disturbance growing out of the
weekly or semi-weekly meetings for the discussion of
sermons, which were the regular diversions of the earnestly theological fathers of the church. Mrs. Hutchinson
followed the example thus set, and instituted meetings of
women for the same purpose, an innovation which, with
her independence of thought and speech, led to great
scandal. With the exception of John Cotton and John
Wheelwright, whom she praised as being under a "covenant of grace," she criticised the ministers of the colony
for being under a "covenant of works." She won large
and influential support, particularly from Governor Vane
and John Cotton; and political parties were formed on the
lines of approval or disapproval of her doctrines. The
triumph of her opponents (guided by John Winthrop and
James Wilson) in the next election led to the calling of a
synod to discuss the sad state of the church. This body
was hostile to Mrs. Hutchinson's party, and its list of
eighty-two heresies involved the utter condemnation of her
opinions. The Boston church excommunicated her, the
magistrates decreed her banishment, certain of her ad-
herents were forced to leave the colony, and many others
were subjected to various penalties and disabilities.[1]

The sentence passed upon him after this submission was that he be disabled
from holding office for three years (*Massachusetts Records*, i. 135, 136; Winthrop, *New England*, i. 185-186, and note). In September, 1636, John Smyth
was banished "for dyvers dangerous opinions, wch hee holdeth, & hath
dyvulged " (*Massachusetts Records*, i. 159).

[1] *Massachusetts Records*, i. 207, 211, 212, 213, 225, 226; Winthrop, *New
England*, i. 239-243, 248-258, 260-265, 267, 268, 278, 282, 284-288, 291-301,
306-312; Palfrey, *New England*, i. 471-521 ; Barry, *Massachusetts*, i. 244-261 ;
Chandler, *Criminal Trials*, i. 1-30; Adams, *Antinomianism in Massachusetts*, and *Three Episodes of Massachusetts History;* Bell, *John Wheelwright.*

Following the treatment of Roger Williams, the outcome of this great Antinomian heresy was the banishment of the spirit of free inquiry.[1] It must be admitted that the opposition party were not contending for the broad principle of freedom of discussion, but merely for the supremacy of their own opinions. One may also explain the reasonableness of the action of the triumphant faction by such considerations as their rights of government, their exclusive proprietary privileges in their territory under the charter, and the necessity of defending themselves against contentious agitators. Nevertheless, the matter must be judged by its results; and from this standpoint the controversy may well be characterized as being in effect a "struggle for freedom of thought and action." There could henceforth be no doubt about the point of view to be taken whenever occasion should require Massachusetts authorities to deal with rights of freedom of discussion in questions involving freedom of the press. They would act upon the familiar principles to which they had been accustomed in England, principles illustrated no less by Star Chamber ordinances than by statutes and by parliamentary special orders and statements of grievances.[2]

[1] Arnold, *Rhode Island*, i. 67.

[2] No attempt has been made to treat all the cases involving the restraint of free discussion before the introduction of printing into Massachusetts. It has seemed unnecessary to do more than sketch a few instances, for the sake of showing clearly the point of view important for this study. Some additional references to various cases, each in some degree illustrating the policy of regulation of opinions and discussion, are the following : *Massachusetts Records*, i. 74, 75, 86, 88, 91, 100; Winthrop, *New England*, i. 67–68.

CHAPTER III.

THE authorities of Massachusetts must have felt the lack of a printing establishment before 1638, both as a matter of convenience for carrying on the government and as a means of promoting learning and religion.[1] The need was supplied by the Rev. Joseph Glover,[2] a wealthy Puritan clergyman, who arranged to bring type, paper, a printing-press, and a printer with him when he started from England in the spring of 1638.[3] Mr. Glover died on the voyage, however, and the difficulties of settling his estate in behalf of his widow and children so delayed the beginning of printing that there were no issues from the press for several months after its arrival in the colony.[4]

[1] Felt (*Annals of Salem*, 2d ed., ii. 9) refers to an expression of this feeling in 1637.

[2] The spelling of Mr. Glover's given name is in dispute. See American Antiquarian Society, *Proceedings*, April, 1875, pp. 5-10.

[3] See Massachusetts Historical Society, *Collections*, 1st series, vii. 19 (quoting Johnson's *Wonder-working Providence*), and *Proceedings*, October, 1895, p. 304; Winthrop, *New England*, i. 348. The bond of Stephen Daye, obliging him to work for Mr. Glover, is printed in Paige's *Cambridge*, 44-45.

[4] Hugh Peters wrote from Salem on October 10, 1638: "We have a printery here, and think to go to work with some special things" (Massachusetts Historical Society, *Collections*, 4th series, vi. 99). Various papers in suits of the Glover heirs, and of Stephen Daye, against President Dunster show that the press was part of the Glover estate. See *Middlesex Court Records* (Mss.), cases cited; Thomas, *History of Printing*, i. 383-390; Quincy, *Harvard University*, i. 187, 459, 466; Andrew McFarland Davis on "The Cambridge Press," in American Antiquarian Society, *Proceedings*, April, 1888, pp. 295-302.

Not until March, 1638–39, did Winthrop record in his journal: "A printing house was begun at Cambridge by one Daye, at the charge of Mr. Glover, who died on sea hitherward. The first thing which was printed was the freemen's oath; the next was an almanac made for New England by Mr. William Peirce, mariner; the next was the Psalms newly turned into metre." [1]

Concerning the status of this first press in Massachusetts, which was also the first in the territory now comprised in the United States, there is a singular absence of information for the period 1639–1641. The maintenance of a press was doubtless an enterprise of public concern favored by the leading men, as Stephen Daye recited in 1657, when he reminded the General Court that he had begun printing at the request of the magistrates and elders.[2] It is probable, also, that in accordance with Puritan principles of government, some simple and direct supervision of scanty issues from the press was maintained by competent authorities, in order to guard against any

---

[1] Winthrop, *New England*, i. 348. Mr. Davis's paper on "The Cambridge Press," noticed above, gives some interesting points about the early issues of this press. The beginning of printing in Massachusetts is commented upon by many authors, as by Peirce, *Harvard University*, 6; Quincy, *Harvard University*, i. 187–188; Thomas, *History of Printing*, i. 14–15, 42–43. See also *Massachusetts Records*, i. 344, iv. pt. i. 306.

[2] See the letter from Hugh Peters, quoted above. See also Thomas, *History of Printing*, i. 45. The official vote of May 15, 1657, was as follows : "Steven Day, of Cambridg, having often complajned that he hath suffered much damage by errecting the printing presse at Cambridge, at the request of the magistrates & elders, for wch he neuer had yett any considerable sattisfaction, this Court doe graunt him three hundred acres of land in any place not formerly graunted by this Court" (*Massachusetts Records*, iv. pt. i. 306). Daye had been allowed such a grant of land as early as December, 1641 (*Ibid.* i. 344). The grant was confirmed in May, 1655, and in May, 1658, Captain Dennison was empowered to lay out the land (*Ibid.* iv. pt. i. 236, 333). Daye was a locksmith by trade, and seems to have turned over the printing to his son Matthew in 1647 (see Paige, *Cambridge*, 44; Massachusetts Historical Society, *Proceedings*, February, 1861, pp. 154–155).

disorders of unrestrained printing.[1] The exact nature,
however, of measures which may have been taken by way
of precautionary control cannot now be ascertained, for
the subject is ignored in all existing contemporary records.

Information upon the status of the press becomes somewhat less dubious after June 22, 1641, when Mr. Glover's
widow became the wife of Henry Dunster, president of
Harvard College, and the control of the Glover estate in
New England passed into the hands of President Dunster.[2] Through his prerogatives as husband and father-
in-law, Mr. Dunster now managed the press, and at the
same time his power as president of the college made him
ex officio the custodian of gifts of type and material for
printing.[3] His respectable and responsible position in the

---

[1] It is possible that there is an example of ordinary censorship in a scanty
record of an incident which occurred in December, 1638. Dudley sent to
Winthrop the copy of a " book " written by Thomas Lechford, saying that he
found "the scope thereof to be erroneous and dangerous, if not hereticall,"
and adding, "I haue sent you the book herewth that in stead of puttinge it to
the presse as hee desireth it may rather be putt into the fire as I desire." See
Massachusetts Historical Society, *Proceedings*, March, 1858, pp. 311-312.
Lechford's own account of his troubles in this connection is found in his note-
book, printed in American Antiquarian Society, *Transactions*, vii. 47-50, 89-90,
440-441. In his concluding statement of due submission to authority was this:
"To cut off all that I desire to your Worships to be pleased to accept of this
my short acknowledgement that I have, I do confess, too far meddled in some
matters of church government and the like which I am not sufficient to understand or declare." For disposition of his case see *Massachusetts Records*, i. 310.

[2] The papers in the case of Appleton *v.* Dunster (*Middlesex Court Records*)
show that Dunster was not legally an executor of the Glover estate, although
he had been actually in possession and enjoyment of that part of it which was
in New England. He was charged with the revenues of the press, even for
the period 1639-1641, before he was president of the college and prior to his
marriage with the Widow Glover. Some additional evidence of his control of
the press is seen in the orders of the General Court, in 1650 and 1654, for printing contracts with " the president." See *Massachusetts Records*, iv. pt. i. 35, 182.

[3] The early gifts of type to Harvard College are recorded as having been
received in 1642 through Mr. Glover and certain gentlemen of Amsterdam.
One entry is open to the construction that the first font of type brought to Cambridge was the property of the college. See *College Book* (Mss.), i. 34, iii. 5.

commonwealth stood as a guarantee of prudent management of the press; and he might certainly have been held accountable for all its publications, even without special order. It is not impossible that the General Court itself may have exercised supervision over the press, since its approval was sought for the printing of sermons[1]; but the absence of formal official control seems attested by the failure of an attempt to establish a board of licensers in May, 1649, as shown by the following document : —

ffor as much as Seuerall inconueniencys may acrew to the Commonwealth by ye liberty of ye pres this Cort doth heerby order y^t noe booke or wrighting shall bee Imprinted w^{th}in this Jurisdiction (exept such questions as are ordinaryly disputed at ye Commensm^ts in ye Colledge ffrom time to time) Vnles they shall be licenced by such psons as are or shall bee appoynted by this Cort for y^t end, : & iff any pson or psons shall imprint or Cause to be imprinted any booke or wrighting with out licence (saue w^t before is exprest) shall therby incur such Censure from this Court as the nature of ye offence shall diserue, & ffurther this Court doth heerby nomminate & authorise : the Gouerner for ye time being — Maior Daniell Dennison & m^r Thomas Sheperd or any two of them to bee licencers of ye pres (during ye pleasure of ye Court)

The deputies haue voted this order desiring our magistrates concurrence heerein.

Edward Rawson, cleric.

The magistrates see no ground to consent wth o^r brethren the deputies heerein.

Jo : Endecott. Gou^r.[2]

---

[1] *Massachusetts Records*, ii. 71. Probably the sermons herein mentioned were not printed : see *Historical Magazine*, February, 1867, p. 116; Colonial Society of Massachusetts, *Publications*, i. 393.

[2] *Massachusetts Archives* (MSS.), lviii. 11. The manuscript contains this additional clause, which was struck out before the order was passed by the deputies : "& w^t euer booke or wrighting shall be licenced vnder ye sd psons

No evidence exists to explain the reasons for the effort of the deputies to enact such a plan as this in Massachusetts, where the magistrates were evidently not apprehensive of any dangers from disorderly printing under existing arrangements. Perhaps the suggestion sprang from the knowledge that measures of like nature were being enforced by their co-religionists who dominated the Long Parliament in England. There the Puritans had destroyed the old agencies for regulating the press, by abolishing the courts of Star Chamber and High Commission in July, 1641.[1] Parliament, however, had speedily supplied new agencies for this important function, by conferring special powers upon its committees,[2] by stimulating the Company of Stationers to active searches and seizures,[3] and by passing orders and ordinances to control printers.[4]

hands or any two of them shall be accoumpted as allowed by this Court." Since there is no date on this paper, it must be determined by internal evidence. It must be before May, 1650, for on and after that date Edward Rawson was secretary of the colony (*Massachusetts Records*, iii. 182); it cannot be before October, 1645, for Daniel Denison did not become a major until after May of that year (*Ibid.* ii. 111). The only year in the interval when John Endicott was governor was from May, 1649, to May, 1650 (*Ibid.* iii. 146). Again, Thomas Shepard died August 25, 1649 (Paige, *Cambridge*, 653). This leaves the conclusion that the order was considered by the General Court at its May session, 1649. It is printed in Massachusetts Historical Society, *Proceedings*, February, 1897, pp. 246–247.

[1] 17 Charles I, cc. 10, 11.

[2] The House of Commons had a Committee for Printing in February, 1641; and before that time a sub-committee of the Grand Committee for Religion had been inquiring into abuses in the licensing and printing of books. Now the new body was " to take into Consideration, and to examine, all Abuses in Printing, Licensing, Importing, and Suppressing of Books of all Sorts; and in denying Licence to some Books, and expunging several Passages out of other Books." See *Commons Journals*, ii. 84; and, for examples of special powers, *Ibid.* 190, 206, 221, 324, 349, 387, 404, 408, 441, 624. See also Rushworth, *Collections*, v. 151.

[3] See *Commons Journals*, ii. 168, 402, 624; Rushworth, *Collections*, iv. 282. Arber (*Transcript*, i. 583–588) prints a contemporary argument that special powers should be given to the company to repress disorders of printing.

[4] On March 9, 1643, the House of Commons authorized the Committee for

The order of June 14, 1643, making stringent but relatively simple provision for the licensing of all printing by parliamentary agents,[1] roused Milton to a noble rebuke of its policy in his " Areopagitica, a Plea for the Liberty of Unlicensed Printing." He urged that the houses should reconsider the order, because it would avail nothing " to the suppressing of scandalous, seditious and libellous Books, which were mainly intended to be supprest," while it would be " primely to the discouragement of all learning, and the stop of Truth, not only by the disexercising and blunting our abilities in what we know already, but by hindring and cropping the discovery that might bee yet further made both in religious and civill Wisdome." Holding that licensing had originated " from the most unchris-

Examinations, or its agents, to search for and seize scandalous and lying pamphlets, and the presses and printers employed upon them. See Husband, *Collections*, 591; *Commons Journals*, ii. 719, 996–997; Arber, *English Reprints: Areopagitica*, 24.

[1] Rushworth, *Collections*, v. 335–336; Scobell, *Ordinances*, pt. i. 44–45; Arber, *English Reprints: Areopagitica*, 25–28. The preamble of the order recited (1) that the bill for regulating printing had been " retarded through the present distractions," until " very many, as well Stationers and Printers, as others of sundry other professions not free of the Stationers Company, have taken upon them to set up sundry private Printing Presses in corners, and to print, vend, publish and disperse Books, pamphlets and papers, in such multitudes, that no industry could be sufficient to discover or bring to punishment, all the severall abounding delinquents ; " and (2) that there had been a general disregard of copyright property interests. It was therefore " Ordered by the Lords and Commons in Parliament, That no Order or Declaration of both, or either House of Parliament shall be printed by any, but by order of one or both the said Houses : Nor other Book, Pamphlet, paper, nor part of any such Book, Pamphlet, or paper, shall from henceforth be printed, bound, stitched or put to sale by any person or persons whatsoever, unlesse the same be first approved of and licensed under the hands of such person or persons as both, or either of the said Houses shall appoint for the licensing of the same, and entred in the Register Book of the Company of Stationers, according to Ancient custom, and the Printer thereof to put his name thereto." Provision was then made for protection of copyright privileges, and for searches and seizures by the master and wardens of the Stationers' Company, the gentleman usher of the House of Peers, the sergeant of the House of Commons, and certain other agents.

tian council and the most tyrannous inquisition that ever inquired," that it "was catcht up by our Prelates, and hath caught some of our Presbyters," Milton warned Parliament that to suppress the "floury crop of knowledge" would be inconsistent with "mild, free and human government," and would be "oppressive, arbitrary, and tyrannous, as they were from whom ye have freed us." Rising to a prophetic expression of an unrealized ideal, he exclaimed, "Give me the liberty to know, to utter, and to argue freely according to conscience, above all liberties."[1] But this plea was addressed to unheeding partisans, since neither the temper of the times nor the spirit of Puritanism could tolerate outspoken arguments and hostile criticism from political and religious antagonists. A restrictive system, only less severe than that administered by the courts of Star Chamber and High Commission,[2] was rapidly developed by numerous direct parliamentary inquisitions against offenders,[3] which were supplemented by more comprehensive legislation in September, 1647.[4]

Massachusetts Puritans could hardly have failed to feel sympathetic appreciation for the spirit and method of such a policy, even if circumstances did not lead them to imitate it fully. They would be strengthened in their principles by their knowledge of the course of events in England, and they would be encouraged to exercise like powers in their own jurisdiction by the later elaborate ordinances of 1649, 1653, and 1655,[5] — measures which reproduced in

---

[1] Milton, *Areopagitica* (Arber, *English Reprints*), *passim.* Although Milton published his pamphlet without a license, no attempt was made to punish him. See Gardiner, *Great Civil War,* ii. 11 ; Masson, *Milton,* iii. 265 ff.

[2] In general, the control of the press by the Long Parliament was somewhat less "thorough" and less successful than the control by the Star Chamber and High Commission had been. See Gardiner, *Great Civil War,* ii. 11.

[3] *Commons Journals,* iii. 315, 457, iv. 296, v. 72, 123, 290.

[4] Scobell, *Ordinances,* pt. i. 134 ; Rushworth, *Collections,* vii. 824.

[5] See Scobell, *Ordinances,* pt. ii. 88–93, 230–231.

detail the system formerly administered against themselves by the ministers of Charles I.

The tendency in Massachusetts to place restrictions upon freedom of discussion is shown by a number of incidents, between 1641 and 1662, which involved the circulation of printed matter and the use of other forms of public agitation. The first of these cases arose from the expression, by the popular party, of dissatisfaction with a proposed "Council for life." Richard Saltonstall, one of the assistants, had written a treatise against the proposal, a paper which was apparently his partisan discussion of a political issue. Governor Winthrop brought some of its passages, which he considered to be "very offensive and unwarrantable," to the attention of the General Court, in May, 1642. The Court's first judgment was that the lack of evil intention in the author should excuse him from any censure; but a month's discussion and reflection led to the conclusion that the standing Council should be vindicated from the reproach cast upon it. The intervention of elders was then invoked with good effect; for they induced Mr. Saltonstall to "ingenuously acknowledge and bewail" his failings, and thereby terminated the incident.[1]

No such fortunate issue marked the series of difficulties which Massachusetts had with Samuel Gorton, — difficulties which present a confused medley of disputes over land titles, rights of jurisdiction, trouble with the Indians, resistance to the authority of magistrates, and contemptuous criticism of the Puritan churches and theology. It is noteworthy, however, that the charges upon which Gorton and his associates were finally arraigned and convicted, in November, 1643, were blasphemy and denial of the civil

---

[1] Winthrop, *New England*, ii. 77–78, 107–109 ; *Massachusetts Records*, ii. 5, 20, 21 ; Hubbard, *New England* (Massachusetts Historical Society. *Collections*, 2d series, vi.), 385–389 ; Felt, *Ecclesiastical History*, i. 473 ; Barry, *Massachusetts*, i. 331–332 ; Palfrey, *New England*, i. 614–616.

authority of Massachusetts. His judges laid great stress upon dangers from his theological opinions, and sentenced him to refrain, on penalty of death, from spreading blasphemous or abominable heresies.[1]

Another religious question which interested New England Congregationalists very deeply was the advance toward legal establishment of the Presbyterian church polity by Parliament. In the literary war waged in England during the sessions of the Westminster Assembly,[2] they were foremost among the opponents of the presbytery. When the temporary triumph of Presbyterianism in Parliament raised the hope of sectaries in Massachusetts, and dangerous books defending toleration and other heresies were in circulation,[3] New England's independence in church matters seemed to be threatened by the exclusive claims of a new hierarchy.[4] Magistrates and elders were extremely sensitive to criticism, and would not permit any person in their jurisdiction openly to question the legality of their local, civil, and ecclesiastical institutions. Nevertheless, a serious agitation for the relaxation of the Massachusetts system of government in church and state began in 1645–46. The magistrates at Plymouth defeated a proposition for "full and free tollerance of religion to all men that would preserve the civill peace"; and the controversy was transferred to Massachusetts.[5] William

---

[1] Winthrop, *New England*, ii. 69–71, 102, 146, 165–169, 171–179, 188–189; *Massachusetts Records*, ii. 41, 44, 46, 51, 52–54; Palfrey, *New England*, ii. 130 ff.; Hazard, *State Papers*, ii. 10 ff.; Janes, *Samuell Gorton;* Gorton, *Simplicities Defence;* Winslow, *Hypocrisie Unmasked.*

[2] Gardiner, *Great Civil War*, ii–iii. *passim;* Dexter, *Congregationalism*, lect. xii.

[3] Winthrop, *New England*, ii. 304; Barry, *Massachusetts*, i. 337; Hubbard, *New England*, 415.

[4] Palfrey (*New England*, ii. 170) says, "The establishment in New England of a civil authority controlled by intolerant Presbyterians would be the establishment of the religious intolerance of that sect."

[5] Hutchinson, *Collections*, 154.

Vassall, Dr. Robert Child, Samuel Maverick, and others petitioned the General Court for a settled form of government according to the laws of England, an extension of the franchise to those not members of approved churches, and admission to recognized church standing of such as were not able to take the church covenants. Coupled with the petition was a threat to appeal to Parliament if the relief prayed for were not given them.

Neglecting this memorial, the General Court called a synod of elders and delegates from all the churches in Massachusetts, Plymouth, New Haven, and Connecticut, to settle the right form of church government and discipline. The "Remonstrance and Petition" of the memorialists was answered within a few months by the General Court in an elaborate "Declaration," published in November, 1646, vindicating the government and laws of Massachusetts and its own proceedings in civil and ecclesiastical affairs. Understanding that the threatened appeal to Parliament was about to be undertaken, the Court arraigned the petitioners for false, scandalous, and seditious representations; but the delinquents refused to answer, denying the jurisdiction of the Court and appealing to England. Heavy fines were then laid upon them, with the effect of stirring them to renewed efforts in the prosecution of their complaints. Child finally succeeded in getting away to England, where he arrived too late to take advantage of the favoring circumstances in Parliament which had given his party hopes of success. The friends of New England were now in the ascendant; and Edward Winslow, the colony's agent, was able to ward off attacks on the independence of Massachusetts. Her ruling minority was not to be interfered with in the policy of governing with a strong hand according to its own ideas; in the phrase of the Cambridge Platform, adopted at the third session of the synod, in 1648, it would continue to restrain offenders from "venting corrupt and pernicious opinions."[1]

The first serious trouble on account of the circulation of printed matter arose in 1650, when "The Meritorious Price of Our Redemption," a theological pamphlet printed in England, but written by William Pynchon, at that time the leading citizen of Springfield and one of the assistants, was received in Boston. The General Court, finding the book to be "erronyous and hereticale," ordered it to be burned by the common executioner in the market-place in Boston, and issued a "Declaration" to prove its own detestation of many of these opinions and assertions, and to show that it was not privy to the publication. The "Declaration" was immediately sent to England to be printed and circulated there, in order that the Court might set itself right with its Christian brethren, while John Norton was entreated to answer Mr. Pynchon's book with all convenient speed, and his answer was also to be sent to England to be printed. Mr. Pynchon was cited to appear before the next General Court to answer for his offence in having violated a law of Massachusetts directed against certain damnable heresies, among which was enumerated any denial that Christ gave himself a ransom for our sins. In his treatment of the price and merit of Christ's sufferings, he had called them "but trials of his obedience, yet intending thereby to amplyfy and exalt the mediatorial

---

[1] Palfrey (*New England*, ii. 166–179) makes out that the movement was nothing but a piece of Presbyterian politics corresponding to the contemporary conditions in England; but Edward Johnson (*Wonder-working Providence*, 202) says of the discontented party that some were "for Prelacy, some for Presbytery, and some for Plebsbytery." Barry (*Massachusetts*, i. 339) describes it as "the most formidable league for the advancement of religious freedom that had yet been witnessed in New England." See also Hutchinson, *Massachusetts*, i. 136–140, and *Collections*, 137, 154, 188–218; *Massachusetts Records*, ii. 154–156, iii. 88, 89, 90–91, 93–94, 113, 114; Child, *New-Englands Jonas;* Winslow, *New-Englands Salamander;* Winthrop, *New England*, ii. 319–321, 340–367.

obedyence of Christ as the only meritorious price of man's redemption," — a dangerous divergence from the received opinion of the elders on a fundamental theological tenet.

Pynchon took counsel of godly ministers, who induced him to make a partial retraction of his errors, and to explain his meaning in a way to take off the worst construction, since he was now "inclined to think that his [Christ's] sufferings were appointed by God for a further end, namely, as the due punishment of our sins by way of satisfaction to divine justice for man's redemption." On receipt of his written statement to this effect, in May, 1651, the General Court conceived that Mr. Pynchon was in a hopeful way to give satisfaction, and granted him more time to consider his position in the light of Mr. Norton's arguments.[1] He was apparently unable to modify his opinions to the desired extent; for, being given further extensions of time in order that he might be led to make a full retraction, he finally escaped prosecution by returning to England, in 1652. Additional interest attaches to his case because Sir Henry Vane intervened by letter to advise the Governor and Council that they ought not to censure any one for matters of a religious nature. Thereupon the Governor and Council vindicated their allegiance to principles of authoritative control, by maintaining that magistrates who abhor a book as pernicious and dangerous are bound to prosecute and punish its author. "We held it our duty," they wrote, "and believed we were called of God to proceed against him." [2]

[1] But he was left out of the magistracy, and was not reëlected as an assistant.

[2] *Massachusetts Records*, iii. 215–216, iv. pt. i. 29–30. The foregoing are the entries of the proceedings in October, 1650, when the book was first condemned. The action was not unanimous, but the "contra dicenting brethren" were not allowed to file their reasons (*Ibid.* iii. 229–230, iv. pt. i. 48–49). Pynchon's written retraction was received and recorded May, 1651. (*Ibid.* iii. 248, 257; and see iv. pt. i. 72, October, 1651). A memoir of

D

The next notable victim of this consistent theory of in-tolerance was Henry Dunster, who had been filling the office of president of Harvard College since 1640, and whose high character and scholarly attainments qualified him in an eminent degree to serve the colony in that capac-ity. The dread of spiritual contamination and the fear of social evils which prompted persecution of the new sect of Anabaptists in Great Britain [1] were likewise operative in the Puritan colonies. Anabaptists had been under the ban in Massachusetts since 1644, when an act denouncing them as " incendiaries of commonwealths" prescribed the penalty of banishment for any person who should openly condemn or oppose the baptizing of infants or secretly " seduce others from the approbation or use thereof." [2] The coming of Clarke, Crandall, and Holmes, three Rhode Island Baptists, to the colony in 1651, threatened to spread doctrines which were believed to be subversive of all social order.[3] Great was the consternation, therefore, when Mr. Dunster became entangled in the " briars of Antipædobap-tism," and followed the leadings of his conscience by bear-ing testimony in some sermons against the administration

Pynchon and an account of his book are given in *New England Historical and Genealogical Register*, xiii. 293; and a more recent sketch of him is in Byington, *The Puritan in England and New England*, 185–218. John Norton's book, *A Discussion of that great Point in Divinity, the Sufferings of Christ*, was published in England in 1653. Mr. Pynchon afterwards pub-lished two answers to Mr. Norton's book, in 1655 and 1662 (see Winsor, *Narrative and Critical History*, iii. 357). A copy of the letter from the Governor and Council to Sir Henry Vane is in *Council Records* (Mss.), i, October 20, 1652; it is printed in Massachusetts Historical Society, *Collec-tions*, 3d series, i. 35–37.

[1] See Gardiner, *England*, and *Great Civil War, passim;* Backus, *History of the Baptists*, i; Dexter, *Congregationalism*, lect. xii.

[2] *Massachusetts Records*, ii. 85, 141, 149; Winthrop, *New England*, ii. 212–214.

[3] Clarke, *Ill Newes from New England;* King, *A Summer Visit of Three Rhode Islanders;* Backus, *History of the Baptists*, i. ch. iv.

of baptism to any infant.[1] Because he disturbed public worship in the Cambridge church by denouncing this ceremony, he was indicted by a grand jury, convicted for breaking the peace, sentenced to receive public admonition on lecture day, and put under bonds to be of good behavior for the future.[2] His official position of course made his dereliction a matter of the greatest concern ; and the General Court therefore voted in May, 1654, that the officers of the college and the selectmen of the towns should not permit any persons who were unsound in doctrine to teach the youth.[3] As President Dunster refused to refrain from teaching his heretical opinions, his resignation from his office was obtained within a few weeks.[4] No more pathetic figure is to be found in the records of Puritanism than this first president of the first American college, who made outspoken opposition to a religious dogma a point of conscience, and who was forced to give up his scholarly service because he felt bound to protest against the rite of infant baptism. His successor in office, Mr. Charles Chauncey, was chosen only after his explicit submission to the restriction that he should not disseminate or publish unsound theories in respect to the mode of baptism and the celebration of the Lord's supper.[5]

The same year that witnessed the deposition of Mr. Dunster brought new cause for anxiety about dissent in Massachusetts, in the appearance in the colony of certain books teaching the tenets of Quakers. The General Court promptly met the emergency by a special vote in these terms : —

---

[1] Mather, *Magnalia*, book iv. ch. iv. § 10.

[2] *Middlesex Court Records*, i. 74 ff.

[3] *Massachusetts Records*, iii. 343–344, 352, iv. pt. i. 182–183.

[4] Quincy, *Harvard University*, i. 17–21.

[5] *Ibid.* 25, 426. Chauncey eventually proved to be not thoroughly orthodox. See below, p. 43.

It is ordred, that all & euery the inhabitants of this jurisdiction that haue any of the bookes in their custody that haue lately bin brought out of England vnder the names of John Reeues & Lodowick Muggleton, who ptend themselvs to be the two last wittnesses & prophets of Jesus Christ, which are full of blasphemies, & shall not bring or send in all such bookes now in their custody, to the next magistř, shall forfeit the sume of ten pounds for euery such booke that shalbe found, or knowne to be in the hands of any inhabitant after one moneths publication hereof, the one halfe to the informer, the other halfe to the country; & as many of the šd bookes as can or may be found *to be* burned by the executior, at Boston.[1]

Two years later, on the arrival of Mary Fisher and Ann Austin as the vanguard of the " Quaker invasion," their books were immediately searched for and seized, the Governor and Council ordering the burning of the books by the executioner. The women were then kept in prison until they could be deported;[2] and notice that similar treatment would be accorded in future to any persons maintaining their opinions was given by the following vote of the General Court: —

And further, it is ordered, if any pson shall knowingly import into any harbor of this jurisdiccon any Quakers bookes or writings concerning theire diuilish opinions, shall pay for euery

---

[1] *Massachusetts Records*, iii. 356. The original order, "voted by yᵉ whole Court" on August 24, 1654, and signed by "Edw. Rawson, Secreᵗʸ," is in *Massachusetts Archives*, lviii. 25.

[2] In *Council Records*, i, under date of July 10, 1656, is the entry of the meeting of the Council "called by the Gounʳ and dept gouernoʳ on the occasion of the Arrival of mary ffisher & Ann : the wife of one Austin." The orders against them, their books, and those who maintained such opinions are recorded in full. See also Neal, *New England*, i. 311–312; A. C. Goodell, in Essex Institute, *Historical Collections*, iii. 243–244. Both quote George Bishop, *New-England Judged.*

such booke or writting, being legally prooved against him or them, the some of five pounds; and whosoeuer shall disperse or conceale any such booke or writing, and it be found w[th] him or her, or in his or her howse, and shall not imedi- ately deliuer in the same to the next magistrate, shall forfeite and pay five pounds for the dispers- ing or concealeing of euery such booke or writing. And it is hereby further enacted, that if any per- son w[th]in this colonje shall take vppon them to defend the hæretticall opinions of the sajd Quak- ers, or any of theire bookes or papers, as afore- sajd, ex annimo, if legally prooved, shallbe fined for the first tjme forty shillings; if they shall persist in the same, and shall so againe defend it, the second tjme fower pounds; if still, notw[th]stand- ing, they shall againe so defend & maintajne the sajd Quakers hæretticall opinions, they shallbe comitted to the howse of correction till there be convenjent passage for them to be sent out of the land, being sentenced by the Court of Asistants to banishment.[1]

Thenceforth it was an essential part of the warfare in Massachusetts against the Quakers to punish severely the importation, concealment, circulation, or defence of their heretical books.[2]

---

[1] *Massachusetts Records*, iv. pt. i. 278 (October, 1656).|

[2] An example of prosecution on suspicion of possession of Quaker books is seen in the case of William Baker, as recorded in *Middlesex Court Records*, i. 145 (December, 1657). The defendant denied that he had any Quaker books; he said that he disliked those which he had seen and had burnt them. In *Massachusetts Records*, iv. pt. ii. 55 (May, 1662), is a record of an action against Captain Robert Lord for bringing in Ann Coleman of the "cursed sect," who "came furnished wth many blasphemous and hæretticall bookes, which she had spread abroad." Paige (*Cambridge*, 345–352) gives particu- lars of the prosecution of one Bowers, a Quaker, and of the burning of one of his books by Mr. Danforth in 1677. These proceedings in Massachusetts were, of course, not essentially different from the persecution of Quakers in European countries and in other English colonies. See Besse, *Sufferings of the Quakers;* Sewel, *History of the Quakers.*

It has been pointed out that a secondary motive in the prosecution of William Pynchon was the fear that failure to repudiate his book might prejudice the colony among its friends in England. A similar consideration was now to bring trouble upon the respected apostle to the Indians, John Eliot, who had written a treatise entitled "The Christian Commonwealth," embodying his speculations upon the nature of the state and the proper form of government. It embraced a fanciful scheme of artificial orders of the people, based upon strained Scriptural analogies; but its essential point was the conclusion that the choice of rulers should be made by election.[1] In 1651 the author, thinking that the time was ripe for putting his plan into operation in the English commonwealth, sent his treatise to some sympathetic Puritan friends in England, where, unluckily for him, it appeared in print in 1659. Had the commonwealth endured, John Eliot's opinions would surely not have incurred censure from Massachusetts; but he had to be sacrificed for the good standing of the colony with the restored Charles II. Massachusetts had enough to answer for without permitting a seeming sanction of views prejudicial to monarchical government to stand as an additional indictment. The General Court, on May 22, 1661, recorded John Eliot's acknowledgment of his errors in "such expressions as doe too manifestly scandalize the goūment of England, by King, Lords, & comōns, as anti Christian, & justify the late innovato^{rs}," and also passed the following order : —

> That the sajd booke be totally suppressed, &
> the authors acknouledgment recorded, and that
> all persons whatsoeuer in this jurisdiction that
> haue any of the sajd bookes in theire custody,

---

[1] *The Christian Commonwealth* is reprinted in Massachusetts Historical Society, *Collections*, 3d series, ix. 127. A copy of the book is in the Carter Brown Library.

shall, on theire perrills, wthin fowerteene dajes
after publication hereof, either cancel & deface
the same, or deliuer them vnto the next magistrate or to the secretary, whereby all farther
divulgment & improovement of the sajd offenciue
booke may be prevented.

And it is further ordered, that Mr Elliots acknowledgement, & the Courts order for the calling in of those bookes, be forthwith transcribed
by the secretary, & caused to be posted vp in
Boston, Charls Toune, Cambridg, Salem, & Ip-
suich, that so all persons concerned therein may
take notice of theire dutjes, & act accordingly.
All wch was done accordingly.[1]

This review of the most significant public controversies
which disturbed the peace of Massachusetts between 1639
and 1662 shows conclusively that there was no recognition
of a general right of freedom of discussion or of a special
right of freedom of the press. There is a temptation to
speak of the "ancient liberty of printing" during the first
generation of Massachusetts history,[2] because one finds no
record of formal censorship for twenty-four years after the
introduction of a printing-press; but the temper of the time
permitted no such liberty in any real sense, and freedom
from supervision by the home government merely allowed
the colony to protect itself from disorderly printing in its
own way. Certainly, exemption from the scrutiny of official licensers did not imply that every man was free to
print whatever he pleased. In all the controversies that
had disturbed the peace since 1639, there is no evidence

[1] *Massachusetts Records*, iv. pt. ii. 5–6. Then follows the transcript of
John Eliot's acknowledgment of his fault. On March 18, 1661, the Governor
and Council had held a session about the book, but had decided to leave the
matter to the General Court. See Felt, *Ecclesiastical History*, ii. 273;
Hutchinson, *Massachusetts*, i. 195–196.

[2] Cf. A. C. Goodell, in Massachusetts Historical Society, *Proceedings*, June,
1893, pp. 271–273.

that even a single issue from the Cambridge press was of
a nature to draw upon the printer or the author the censure of the magistrates. Almanacs, theses, religious tracts,
and books in the Indian tongue, laws and other official
publications, a few sermons of approved orthodoxy, editions of the Psalms, a life of John Cotton, — these make
up the limited list of books issued down to 1662.[1] Dis-
creet supervision by President Dunster and by President
Chauncey made formal censorship quite unnecessary.

---

[1] For lists of titles, see Thomas, *History of Printing*, ii. 309–314; Green,
on " Early American Imprints," in Massachusetts Historical Society, *Proceedings*, February, 1895, pp. 415–417; Paine, on the same subject, in American
Antiquarian Society, *Proceedings*, October, 1895, pp. 281–288; Evans, *American Bibliography*, i. 1–15.

CHAPTER IV.

RESTRICTIVE CENSORSHIP, 1662–1685.

THE year 1662 marked a time of great anxiety for Massachusetts.[1] The restoration of the Stuarts had given favorable opportunities to many enemies of the colony to prosecute their complaints; and the necessity of endeavoring to placate triumphant opponents, while yet maintaining orderly government according to Puritan ideas, made the government's course a difficult one to steer. Especial precautions had to be taken against the expression of opinions offensive to the court party in England;[2] while by the uncertainties of their political existence the magistrates were made unusually sensitive to anything like "contempt of authority." Besides the irritation of external pressure, the boldness of the Quakers, stimulated by royal commands for the cessation of persecution, and the dissensions over the synod and its "halfway covenant," were a serious menace to internal peace.[3]

It was under such circumstances that the General Court, in October, 1662, passed the first formal act for restrictive censorship of the press in Massachusetts, in the following terms : " For prevention of irregularitjes & abuse to the authority of this country by the printing presse, it is ordered, that henceforth no copie shall be printed but by

[1] See Barry, *Massachusetts*, i. 381–386; Palfrey, *New England*, ii. 520–530.

[2] The General Court in October, 1662, considered the king's letter and ordered it to be published. See *Massachusetts Records*, iv. pt. ii. 58.

[3] See cases before the General Court in May and October, 1662, involving prosecutions for sedition and " contemptuous carriage " toward magistrates.

the allowance first had & obteined under the hands of Capt̄ Daniel Gookin & Mʳ Jonathan Mitchel, vntil this Court shall take further order therein." [1]

The only printing establishment in the colony at this time, and therefore the only one to which the new order then applied, was that belonging to Harvard College, maintained in Cambridge, and consisting of two presses with their equipments. One of these was the Glover press, which had been sold to the college by President Dunster in 1654, when he was forced to resign.[2] The other was a recent acquisition from the Corporation for the Propagation of the Gospel among the Indians, placed for use in the college printing-office by the Commissioners of the United Colonies.[3] Both presses were under the responsible over-

---

[1] *Massachusetts Records*, iv. pt. ii. 62.

[2] See Davis on "The Cambridge Press," in American Antiquarian Society, *Proceedings*, April, 1888, p. 297.   In an inventory of the estate of Harvard College taken December 10, 1654, are the following items : —

" One small house unfinished, intended for a printing house."

" A printing press, with all its appurtenances, now in the occupation of Samuel Green Printer, the pʳticulars whereof are expressed in an Inventory given in by the sᵈ Printer to the Presidⁿᵗ vallued the whole at eighty pounds " (*College Book*, Mss., iii. 41, 42, 47).

The corporation, explaining the needs of the college on May 9, 1655, represented that " the Revenue of yᵉ Presse (wᶜʰ is but Small) must at present be improved for yᵉ finishing of yᵉ Print-house : its Continuance in yᵉ Presidᵗˢ house being (besides other Inconveniences) dangerous & hurtfull to yᵉ edifice thereof " (*Massachusetts Archives*, lviii. 32).

[3] Mr. Usher, agent for the commissioners, had purchased a press, type, etc., in England at the expense of the corporation (see *Plymouth Records*, x. 240).   This action was doubtless a result of representations in the following petition (*Massachusetts Archives*, lviii. 37) : —

" To the Honoʳᵉᵈ Generall Court assembled
at Boston, the Jnformation & request of Samuel
Green, Printer at Cambridge

" Humbly sheweth

" Whereas yoʳ poare Servant hath (althovgh with many wants & difficultyes) spent some yeares in attending yᵉ service of yᵉ Country in that worke of printing, The Presse & the appurtenances thereof, wᵗhout a speedy svpply,

sight of President Chauncey, who had held his position for
nearly six years, and against whom there had been no
complaints of dereliction of duty in permitting disorderly
printing, — facts which cast doubt upon the sufficiency of
the merely general reasons stated in the order for the
innovation of appointing licensers of the press. " Irregu-
larities and abuse to the authority of this country " would
certainly be feared in the midst of uncertainties about
political and religious status; but why should there be a
departure from a method of control over the press which
experience had justified in practice ? A possible answer
to this question is suggested by President Chauncey's
position in the controversy over the " halfway covenant."
Chauncey had joined with Increase Mather and John
Davenport in leading the minority party in its opposition
to the adoption of that theological compromise, a step
which may have aroused distrust of his discretion, and
made some other method of control seem advisable.[1]

& y^t especially of letters, & those principally for ye printing of English, is
now almost wholly vncapeable of farther improvem^t, either for the answer-
ing of ye Countryes expectation, or for the benefitt of such as are employed
therein, & ye Colledge (to whome ye presse doth pperly belong), have not
ability in theyr hands to helpe, so that vnlesse some p^rsent care bee taken by
the wisdome & furtherance of this Hon^rd Court, ye improvem^t thereof must
of necessity cease, & yor poore servant must bee forced to change either his
habitation or employm^t or both. The consideration & supply whereof is the
humble request of yor poore servant, or if not, yor determination therein, y^t so
hee may more clearely see his way for ye serving of the pvidence of god in
some other calling.

" In answer to this pet. the deputyes Conceiue the Consideration hereof
should be Commended to the Comission^rs of the vnited Colonyes at their
next meetinge that so they may write to the Corporation in england if they
se meet for the pcureing of 20^li worth of letters for the vse of the Jndian
Colledge the deputyes haue passt this & desire o^r hon^rd magis^ts Consent heerto

" William Torrey Cleric

" Consented to by ye magis^ts

" 5 June 1658

" Edw. Rawson Secret^y "

[1] Felt (*Ecclesiastical History*, ii. 288–302) gives notes as to the synod, the
action of the minority, and the treatment of the dissenters, which make clear

An alternative conjecture is connected with the career of Marmaduke Johnson, the able printer sent from England to assist in the great work of printing for the Indians.[1] Mr. Johnson was not a well-behaved person. In April, 1662, he was indicted for " alluring the daughter of Samuel Green, printer, and drawing away her affections without the consent of her father," as well as for making threats against the life of any man who should pay addresses to her. For winning the affections of the young woman, he was fined five pounds; for his threatening speeches, he was put under bonds to keep the peace; for his attempt to marry when he had a wife in England, he was ordered to return to the mother country.[2] The execution of the order of banishment was deferred for two years; but it may be supposed that this troublesome printer seemed to have a power for mischief which needed to be checked before he should do any harm.

Mere colonial respect for the procedure of the mother country may have suggested the constitution of a board of licensers of the press. The legislation of the common-wealth régime in England had indeed lapsed upon the restoration of Charles II, and decrees of Star Chamber and High Commission courts were no longer available for the regulation of printing. Nevertheless, the king had par-tially assumed that function by virtue of his general pre-

---

the uncertainty felt about Chauncey, Davenport, Increase Mather, and other church leaders. It was counted a great gain that the minority was not for-bidden to print its dissenting opinions. For doubts as to the actual printing of the dissenting judgment in Massachusetts in 1662, see Green and Paine on " Early American Imprints," in Massachusetts Historical Society, *Proceed-ings*, February, 1895, p. 418, and American Antiquarian Society, *Proceedings*, October, 1895, p. 288.

[1] For articles of agreement between Johnson and the Corporation in Eng-land, see *Plymouth Records*, x. 447–449.

[2] Paige, *Cambridge*, 594; Thomas, *History of Printing*, i. 76–79; *Middle-sex Court Records*, i; *Massachusetts Records*, iv. pt. ii. 93.

rogative, and with the implied sanction at least of his Parliament, Sir John Birkenhead being appointed licenser.[1] During the revolutionary period, not only ephemeral pamphlets and news-letters, but periodical newspapers, had become common as a means of public discussion and agitation. There was apparent need, therefore, for the legislative enactment of a comprehensive licensing system, since " the well-government and regulating of printers and printing-presses is matter of publick care, and of great concernment, especially considering, that by the general licentiousness of the late times, many evil disposed persons have been encouraged to print and sell heretical, schismatical, blasphemous, seditious and treasonable books, pamphlets and papers, and still do continue such their unlawful and exorbitant practice, to the high dishonour of Almighty God, the indangering the peace of these kingdoms, and raising a disaffection to his most excellent Majesty and his government: for prevention whereof, no surer means can be advised, than by reducing and limiting the number of printing-presses, and by ordering and settling the said art or mystery of printing by act of parliament." [2] A disagreement between the houses over certain points of detail caused the defeat of a bill of this kind in 1661 ; [3] but the measure was passed in May, 1662.[4]

---

[1] The House of Commons petitioned the king, in 1660, to issue a proclamation to suppress books by Milton and Goodwin (see *Commons Journals*, viii. 66). The printing of votes or proceedings without leave was denounced as a breach of privilege, and a committee was promptly instructed to consider and advise what should be done for regulating printing (*Ibid.* 74, 80, 134). Birkenhead held his position as licenser from November, 1660, to August, 1663, a period including regulation by purely executive power and control under statutory sanction.

[2] Preamble of 13 & 14 Charles II, c. 33.

[3] *Commons Journals*, viii. 288, 312, 313, 314, 315, 316.

[4] While the bill for regulating the press was pending in the Commons, the king sent a message to urge its speedy passage, asserting that, next to the bill for settling the forces of the kingdom, this measure " did most conduce to the

This statute, known as 13 & 14 Charles II, chapter 33, supplemented the common-law right of the crown to regulate the press, by express provisions framed on the model of Star Chamber and commonwealth ordinances, and covering nearly every possible contingency of control. The vital principle of such a law consisted in the requirement that restrictive censorship by official licensers should be the almost universal rule: except governmental and university publications, nothing was to issue from the press in England without previous authorization from these licensers. At the same time the number of presses, master printers, workmen, and apprentices was carefully limited; and the system as a whole aimed at the most perfect protection of the government and the community from disorders of unsupervised and irresponsible printing.[1] The Massachusetts measure certainly resembled in spirit, and may have been designed to be a simplified copy of this English system.[2]

Whatever may have been the determining reasons for the passage of the licensing act of October, 1662, conditions must have changed rapidly; for the next General Court, meeting May 27, 1663, passed the following order: —

> Itt is ordered that the printing presse be at liberty as formerly, till this Court shall take further order, & the late order is heereby repealed.[3]

securing the Peace of the Kingdom; the exorbitant Liberty of the Press having been great Occasion of the late Rebellion in the Kingdom, and Schisms in the Church" (*Ibid.* 425).

[1] The administration of this act and the activity of Roger L'Estrange as licenser are noticed in Bourne, *English Newspapers*, i. 32–42.

[2] The first section of this act also applied in terms to "any other his Majesties dominions, or in the parts beyond the seas." Yet there is no evidence that it was invoked or cited in any colonial regulation of "heretical, seditious, schismatical or offensive books or pamphlets," except in the prosecution of William Bradford in Pennsylvania in 1692. There the prosecuting attorney cited the clause requiring that a printer should put his name on everything he printed. See Thomas, *History of Printing*, i. 219.

[3] *Massachusetts Records*, iv. pt. ii. 73.

Here again the absence of any contemporary statement of reasons for the legislative policy leaves scope for conjectural explanation.[1] Perhaps time had demonstrated that there was nothing to fear from Marmaduke Johnson. It is not improbable, too, that the new method of control had been found cumbersome and inconvenient, and that confidence in President Chauncey as governor of the press was restored, if it had ever been really impaired.[2]

Prior to May, 1665, there was no strictly private commercial ownership of a press in Massachusetts; but in that month Marmaduke Johnson returned from a trip to England, bringing with him a full equipment for a printing establishment of his own. Despite his reputation for disorderly conduct, Mr. Johnson had been permitted to remain in Cambridge for the completion of his contracts to work on the Indian printing, or until August, 1664.[3] This indulgence was won for him by the intercession of his friend John Eliot, and by the consideration of the General Court for his employers, the honorable Corporation for the Propagation of the Gospel among the Indians. Returning now to the scene of his former labors when no law existed for the control of such a business as his or for oversight of his publications, Mr. Johnson sought the best location for his printing-office. He concluded that it would prosper most in Boston, and accordingly applied to the selectmen of that town for permission to become an inhabitant in order that he might establish his business in the metropolis.[4]

[1] Drake (*Boston*, i. 366) says that Mr. Gookin and Mr. Mitchell "would allow of no printing at all," an assertion that is manifestly inaccurate. Cf. Thomas, *History of Printing*, ii. 314.

[2] President Chauncey was a member of the board of censors established in May, 1665. See below, p. 48.

[3] *Massachusetts Records*, iv. pt. ii. 93.

[4] Search in the publications of the Boston Record Commissioners for any mention of these facts has been vain; but they may be accepted on the testimony of Mr. Johnson himself, as given in a petition of 1668. See below, p. 50.

At this juncture, to meet a new emergency, the General Court took action as follows: —

> For the preventing of irregularitjes & abuse to the authority of this country by the printing presse, It is ordered by this Court & the authority thereof, that there shall be no printing presse allowed in any toune w^{th}in this jurisdiction but in Cambridge, nor shall any person or persons presume to print any copie but by the allowance first had & obteyned vnder the hands of such as this Court shall from tjme to tjme impower; the præsident of the colledge, Mr John Shearman, Mr Jonathan Michell, & Mr Thomas Shepheard, or any two of them, to survey such copie or coppies, and to prohibitt or allow the same according to this order; and in case of non observance of this order, to forfeit the presse to the country, & be disabled from vsing any such proffession w^{th}in this jurisdiction for the tjme to come; provided, this order shall not extend to the obstruction of any coppie which this Court shall judge meete to order to be published in print.[1]

[1] *Massachusetts Records,* iv. pt. ii. 141 ; Massachusetts Historical Society, *Proceedings,* February, 1897, p. 243. Manuscript copies of the vote are in *Massachusetts Archives,* lviii. 55. As it passed the deputies the first time, it named the licensing board in the following terms : —

"& for the p^rsent doe nominate & empowre Capt Daniel Gookin m^r Tho: Danforth the p^rsent p^rsident of the Colledge & m^r Jonathan Michell or any three of them."

The magistrates acted upon it thus : —

"Consented vnto pvided that instead of Capt Daniell Gookin and m^r Tho: Danforth m^r John Shearman and m^r Tho. Shepherd be deputed to Joyne wth the p^rsent p^rsedent and m^r Jonathan Mitchell any two of whome shall haue power to allowe or phibit printing according to this order

"Consented to by ye depu^{ts}

                              " Ri : Bellingham Govr

                              " William Torrey Cleric "

Most of the books that mention this licensing order put it in 1664 (*e.g.,* Winsor, *Memorial History of Boston,* i. 456), a mistake which arose from the fact that the act was entered at the end of the records of the October session of 1664. A marginal note in *Massachusetts Records* gives the right date.

Thus Massachusetts again adopted the method of control over printing which was normal in English experience,[1] being compelled to take such action by Marmaduke Johnson's enterprise; and henceforth this policy was to prevail, with only slight modifications, throughout the continuance of government under the colony charter. Some significance, however, attaches to various incidents of its operation which must receive explanation.

After a two years' trial of the licensing régime, an effort was made to secure relaxation of the more stringent features of the system. In May, 1667, the Council passed an amended order, permitting the setting up of presses anywhere in the jurisdiction, and requiring licenses only for books or papers designed for public sale. Instead of subjecting an offending printer to the heavy penalty of the law of 1665, — that is, to forfeiture of his press, and disability "from using any such profession within this jurisdiction for the time to come," — this order provided that non-observance of its regulations would incur merely forfeiture of all the impressions of unlicensed publications, besides liability to a fine of five pounds for each offence. The deputies were not willing to consent to the passage of the proposed order, and it failed to become a law.[2]

---

[1] Renewals of the English act of 13 & 14 Charles II, c. 33, were made by 16 Charles II, c. 8; 16 & 17 Charles II, c. 7; 17 Charles II, c. 4. Sir Roger L'Estrange was appointed active "surveyor of the press" (*Calendar of State Papers, Domestic,* 1661–1662, p. 282 ff.). He was to have the sole privilege of writing, printing, and publishing all manner of news matter; and the official *London Gazette* became the only authorized vehicle of intelligence (*Ibid.* 1663–1664, p. 240 ff.).

[2] *Massachusetts Archives,* lviii. 57; Massachusetts Historical Society, *Proceedings,* February, 1897, p. 247. The text of the proposed measure was as follows: —

"It is orderd by this court & the authority therof: that no printer within this Jurisdiction shall p'sume to imprint any booke or paper, for publike sale, vnles the same be alowed vnder the hands of m' Charls Chancy m' John Sheman pastour of waterton m' Jonathan michel pastor of cambridge m' Tho

E

Because of the importance of Boston as the commercial and political capital, the requirement that there should be no press allowed outside of Cambridge was a serious hindrance to the business of the printers. The last-mentioned attempt to secure the removal of this restriction having failed, Marmaduke Johnson now addressed the General Court in the following self-explanatory argumentative petition : —

> To the hono^{ble} the Govern^r, the Deputy Govern^r, and the rest of the Honored Magistrats, & deputies of the Masachusets Collony Assembled in the Generall Court at Boston. 29th 2mo 1668
>
> The humble petition of Marmaduke Johnson of Cambridge, Printer.
>
> Sheweth,
>
> That yor petitioner by the good hand & providence of God returning from England in the year 1665. with his printing press, & letters, and finding no law of the Country, nor order of any Court to prohibit ye Exercise of his calling in any town, or place convenient within this Jurisdiction, did apply himself (according to the Custome of strangers) to the select men of the Town of Boston, for their admittance of him into that town to inhabit : In which Juncture of time, yor petitioner was informed that an order had passed this Hon^{r}ed Court, prohibiting the Exercise of printing in any town within this Jurisdiction, save only at Cambridge. Whereupon yor petitioner did yeild ready obedience thereunto, and tooke Cam-

Shepard teacher of charles towne or any 2 of them; vpon the penalty of forfeture of all the imp^{r}sion : to bee seased on by warrant from one or 2 magistrates & the fine of fiue pounds : to be payd by the printer for euery offenc being herof Legaly conuicted.

"The magis^{ts} haue past this wth Refference to the Consent of their bretheren the deputjes heereto

"Edw: Rawson Secre^{ty}
the debutys consntd not herto
Richard Waldern Speker"

"21th of may 1667
"27: 3: 1667

bridge for his place of abode, where he hath ever since continued. Now may it please this hon^{red} Court, yor petitioner finding to his great loss & Detriment the inconveniency of living in a town where no trade, or very little is managed, especially in that which is appertaining to, or tends to the promotion of his calling, as yor petitioner is ready more fully to demonstrate if called thereunto, and being desirous by all lawfull ways & means to make himself, and his art as usefull and advantagious to this Commonwealth as possibly he may, by Gods blessing on his indeav^{rs}: And humbly conceiving that there is not the like restraint, or confinement of any other art, or science :

Doth therefore in all humillity pray & beseech this hon^{red} Court, that you would be pleased to take the premises into yor grave & serious Considerations, that so (if in yor wisdomes you shall see meet) the practitioners of the art of Printing may have liberty to sit down in such convenient place within this Jurisdiction, as they shall finde most commodious for them ; Submitting at all times to all such laws & orders as are, or shall be made concerning the premises, by the Authority of this Comonwealth.

And yor Petitioner (as in duty bound) shall ever pray. &c.

The unfavorable action of the General Court upon **Mr.** Johnson's plea is indorsed on the original document **in** these terms : —

The magis^{ts}. Judge it not Convenient to grant the peticoners request their brethrenn the deputyes hereto Consenting
12 May 1668   Edw: Rawson, Secre^{ty}
The deputyes Consent hereto
                William Torrey Cleric,
The deputyes haue further voted that the pet^r should haue his money he payd for entry

of his pet. returned agayne wth refference to the
consent of o^{r} Hono^{rd} magists hereto
                                    William Torrey Cleric.[1]

Later in the same year, and perhaps as a result of the continued restraint and limitation of his business, Mr. Johnson
fell into temptation, and broke the law requiring license for
all publications.   It was on September 2, 1668, that Edward
Rawson, as secretary to the Council, issued warrants to
Marshal Nicholson directing him to summon Samuel
Green and Marmaduke Johnson, printers, to make their
personal appearance before the Council, prepared to give
account of what books they had printed lately, and by
what authority.   The examinations showed that Mr. Green
had obtained due license for all his recent issues, seven in
number, but that Mr. Johnson had failed to get allowance
for one of his five publications.[2]   Upon conviction for his
offence, he pleaded thus, in another petition, for indulgent
treatment : —

> To the honorable Councill of the Comonwealth.
> The humble Petition of Marmaduke Johnson of
> Cambridge, Printer.
>   Sheweth,
>   That yor Petition^{r} doth with all humility ac-
> knowledge his rashness & inadvertency in printing
> a late pamphlett (called, The Isle of Pines) with-
> out due Order & License first had & obtain'd;
> for which being summoned before this honorable
> Councill, upon his Confession & Conviction, was
> fined in the sum of five pounds to the Comon-
> wealth.   Now may it please this honoured Coun-
> cill, yor Petition^{r} having in that act no intent or
> design to contemn Authority, or to vend or publish

---

[1] *Massachusetts Archives,* lviii. 58; Massachusetts Historical Society, *Proceedings,* February, 1897, pp. 244–245.

[2] *Massachusetts Archives,* lviii. 59–60; Massachusetts Historical Society,
Proceedings, February, 1897, pp. 247–248.

any thing that might be displeasing thereto (as may appear by his affixing his Name to the said Pamphlett) but only the hope of procuring something to himself thereby for his necessary subsistence; his Calling in this Country being very chargeable, his living thereon difficult, the gain thereby vncertain, & his losse by printing frequent: He therefore prayes this honoured Councill, (if it may seem good to yo[r] wisdomes) that the said fine may be remitted vnto him, & he discharged from the payment thereof.

And yo[r] pet[r] shall ever pray &c.[1]

Mr. Johnson was not alone in his dissatisfaction with the state of the printing trade in Cambridge. In the following humble request, his business rival endeavored, but in vain, to get some relief from his difficulties: —

To the Honoured Councill sitting att Boston
the Humble request of Samuel Green printer to the Colledge att Cambridge:
Humbly intreateth that whereas there was an Order made by the Honoured Generall Court Concerning printing: that there should be no printing; but att Cambridge; and that what was printed there should be approved by those four Gentlemen appointed by the Court then, or any two of them, yo[r] Worships would please to explaine whether it is required those Gentlemen that allow of the printing of what is presented, should sett to their hands as Imprimators to it; as also when they express there shall be no printing but att Cambridg, whether they intend that any one may sett up printing, provided it be in that town, or any part of it; or whether they intend that the printing be onely under the in-

---

[1] *Massachusetts Archives*, lviii. 63; Massachusetts Historical Society, *Proceedings*, February, 1897, p. 249. The documents contain no answer to this plea for clemency; nor do they explain why the full penalty of the law, which provided for the forfeiture of the offender's press and for disability to continue his business, was modified.

spection of the Colledge there; if there be libertie for any to sett up printing in the limitts of that Town that they would please to make such orders concerning it, that one may not wrong another by printing anothers Copie when he hath been att charge about it, as it is in other places where severall printing houses are: for some of us do find a need of such things already, although there is but worke little inough for one printing house, to the great discouragement of yor poor serv$^{t:}$ in the place whereto he hath been called and hitherto to his poor abillitie hath endeavoured to be faithfull in it, according to what hath been required

And yor Serv$^{t:}$ Shall ever pray:

Cambr: Octob: 14: (68)[1]

The magistrates had proved in no uncertain manner that they were not content simply to create a board of licensers for nominal oversight of the press, but that they meant to enforce the regulations and were not willing to relax them. Moreover the General Court did not abandon its watchful care against the printing of obnoxious books. In May, 1669, on information that a reprint of "The Imitatation of Christ," by Thomas à Kempis, was in press, it intervened to direct the licensers to revise the work more fully, and to order that meanwhile there should be no further progress in the work.[2] The first modification of this rigorous system was made five years later, upon the sole point of permitting the establishment of a printing-

[1] *Massachusetts Archives*, lviii. 60; Massachusetts Historical Society, *Proceedings*, February, 1897, p. 251. No answer to this request for information and for a copyright law has been found. The first order for anything like copyright was passed in May, 1672, at the request of John Usher. See *Massachusetts Records*, iv. pt. ii. 527.

[2] *Massachusetts Records*, iv. pt. ii. 424. In October, 1669, New Plymouth ordered its election sermon of the previous June to be printed, and on December 8 recorded that this had been done " by the approbation alsoe of Mr Chauncye and Mr Shepard, whoe alsoe aded imprimature thervnto as it is now extant " (*Plymouth Records*, v. 30).

office in Boston. Once more Marmaduke Johnson came forward to present the reasonable and moderate demands of his business interests. The original document here reproduced gives his straightforward account of the circumstances, as well as of the resulting action : —

To the hon^ble^ the Governo^r^, Deputy Governo^r^, & the rest of the hon^d^ : Magistrates & Deputies for the Massachusetts Colony, assembled in Generall Court at Boston, 27 : 3^d^ Moneth, 1674.

The humble Petition of Marmaduke Johnson of Cambridge, Printer :

Sheweth,

That yor pet^r^ being in London brought up in the Art of Printing, & in no other Calling or Occupation; & being by the Providence of God brought into this Country with his Press & Letters in the year 1665. It pleased this hon^d^ Court (after his arrivall) to pass an Order bearing date the 3^d^ of May in the year aforesaid, thereby prohibiting the exercise of Printing in any Town within this Jurisdiction, save only at Cambridge : In obedience wherevnto yor pet^r^ hath ever since made that his place of residence. But finding by long & sad Experience the great discomodity & detriment by such Confinement of his Calling, & an absolute impossibility of providing comfortably for himself & family by the Incomes thereof, though managed with greatest Care, & followed with all possible diligence, not having imployment therein for one third part of his time, Conflicting with difficulties too great & many to be here recited : And also being sensible of the loss & disadvantage accrewing hereby to the Comonwealth, who by his Art & Endeavo^rs^ might have many vsefull & profitable Tracts printed & published here, were he allowed the liberty of his Calling in a convenient place of Trade : And humbly conceiving, no more security to the State, in preventing the printing things irregular, or abusive therevnto, by such Confinement, then if it were exercised in the most popul[ous] Town within this Jurisdiction; all which yor pet^r is ready to demonstrate, if called therevnto:

Doth therefore in all humility pray this hon^d Court, That you would be pleased to take the premises into yor grave & serious Considerations, & grant him such liberty & relief therein as in yor wisdoms shall seem meet; that so the Art of Printing may by this hono^d: Court be duely incouraged, & the practition^{rs} thereof have Lawfull liberty of exercising the same in such place within this Jurisdiction, as they shall finde most comodious for them, & most to the advantage of the Comonwealth; submitting at all times to such Laws & Orders as are or shall be made concerning the premises, by the Authority of this Comonwealth.

And yor pet^r (as in duty bound shall ever pray &c.

Marmaduke Johnson.

30th may 1674:

The magis^{ts}. Judge meet to grant the peticoners request. so as nothing be printed till licenc be obteyned according to lawe their Brethren the deputyes hereto Consenting

Edw. Rawson, Secre^{ty}

The deputyes Consent hereto

William Torrey Cleric.[1]

The General Court supplemented the granting of this petition by providing additional agents for licensing, in these terms: —

Whereas there is now granted that there may be a printing press elswhere then at Cambridge, for the better regulation of the press, it is ordered and enacted, that the Reuerend Mr Thomas Thatcher & Mr Increase Mather, of Boston, be added vnto the former licensers, and they are hereby impowred to act accordingly.[2]

---

[1] *Massachusetts Archives*, lviii. 91; Massachusetts Historical Society, *Proceedings*, February, 1897, pp. 245-246.   [2] *Massachusetts Records*, v. 4.

Mr. Johnson lived but a few months to enjoy his privileges in Boston, and then Mr. John Foster, a graduate of Harvard, became the proprietor of the only Boston press.[1] So free were the ensuing seven years from all disturbances on account of disorderly printing,[2] that the occasional

[1] Some perplexing questions arise in connection with the granting of Marmaduke Johnson's petition and the identity of the first Boston printer. It has been claimed that John Foster was the first one (see Thomas, *History of Printing*, i. 84; Winsor, *Memorial History of Boston*, i. 456; Sibley, *Harvard Graduates*, ii. 222). "Government," says Thomas, "now authorized Foster to set up a press in Boston."

It must have been necessary for Foster to get permission to set up his press; but no record of that permission can be found, unless the granting of Marmaduke Johnson's petition may be counted as a general allowance to any person to set up his press in Boston or in any other town in the jurisdiction. So far as appears from the records, however, the permission given to Johnson was intended to be personal and specific, and was not a general order. Shortly after the favorable result of his petition, Johnson was elected "college printer" (*Sewall Papers*, i. 3), an action probably taken with the hope of retaining in Cambridge the only well-trained printer in the colony; but he removed to Boston, and lived there until his death, December 25, 1674 (Paige, *Cambridge*, 594; Boston Record Commissioners, *First Report*, 1876, p. 54; *Suffolk Wills*, Mss., book v. 227). The facts, therefore, seem to warrant the conclusion that Marmaduke Johnson, not John Foster, was the first Boston printer.

[2] The Massachusetts Historical Society, in its *Collections*, 5th series, i. 420–421, 422–424, prints two letters from Samuel Green, Sr., to John Winthrop, Jr., which throw some light upon the conditions of the printing trade in 1674–75. The first of these letters, dated July 8, 1674, begs payment for the printing of the Connecticut laws by Green two years before. The second, dated July 6, 1675, is a recital of Green's "aggrivances." He says that he took up printing unwillingly on the death of Day (Matthew Day), because urged to it; that all went well until Marmaduke Johnson came over and became angry over the love affair with Green's daughter; that Johnson then went to England, brought back type and a press, and "wrought me," he adds, "quite out of the Indian worke." He goes on to say that, on Johnson's death the preceding winter, he bought his type, the part belonging to the corporation in England having been directed to be turned over to the college. Mr. Eliot and Mr. Stoughton, he continues, "put them into the hand of a young man [John Foster?] that had no skill of printing but what he had taken notice by the by, and the Indian worke is all putt into his hand, and I and my son altogether defeated." So Green asks Winthrop to write to the corporation to straighten the matter out, that he may get the type and the Indian work.

filling of vacancies in the board of licensers gives the only notice of its existence.[1]

Massachusetts, as a colonial government acting under its own local laws, was not obliged to amend them to conform to the developments of the internal policy of the mother country. Therefore the expiration of the English licensing acts by limitation in 1679, when Charles II dissolved Parliament and left the press in England temporarily free from statutory restrictive censorship, seems to have had no effect upon the Massachusetts system. The crisis in the mother country had been met through a common-law doctrine, thus stated by Chief-Justice Scroggs: "When, by the king's command, we were to give in our opinion, what was to be done in point of the regulation of the press; we did all subscribe, that to print or publish any news-books or pamphlets of news whatsoever, is illegal; that it is a manifest intent to the breach of the peace, and that they may be proceeded against by law for an illegal thing. Suppose now that this thing is not scandalous, what then? If there had been no reflection in this book at all, yet it is *illicite*, and the author ought to be convicted for it." [2]

---

[1] From the institution of regular licensers to the end of the colonial charter period, appointments were made as follows: —

October, 1662, Daniel Gookin and Jonathan Mitchell (*Massachusetts Records*, iv. pt. ii. 62; order for appointment repealed May, 1663, *Ibid.* 73).

May, 1665, President Chauncey, John Shearman, Jonathan Mitchell, Thomas Shepard (*Ibid.* 141).

May, 1672, John Oxenbridge and Urrian Oakes, added to the board of licensers on the death of President Chauncey (*Ibid.* 509).

May, 1674, Thomas Thatcher and Increase Mather, on granting Marmaduke Johnson's petition (*Ibid.* v. 4).

May, 1675, James Allin, on the death of John Oxenbridge (*Ibid.* 32).

Special licensers were sometimes appointed for important publications, as is shown by the case of Hubbard's *Narrative of the Troubles with the Indians*, which contains a license signed by Simon Bradstreet, Daniel Denison, and Joseph Dudley. They spoke of themselves as deputed by the Governor and Council to "peruse and license"; and the book was "published by authority."

[2] Rex *v.* Carr, *State Trials*, vii. 1127.

The application of this doctrine in England, in libel prosecutions, controlled the press almost as effectively as the licensing system itself had done; but the continued maintenance of censorship in Massachusetts gave such satisfaction that, by the time Mr. Foster died, in September, 1681, the authorities were so impressed with the obvious safety and convenience of having a press in Boston that their tone with respect to tolerating one there was quite changed. The circumstances and the feeling of the time are shown in the following extract from the records of the General Court, in October, 1681 : —

> M[r] Samuel Seawall, at the instance of some freinds, wth respect to the accomodation of the publicke, being prevajled with to vndertake the mannagement of the printing press in Boston, late vnder the improovement of M[r] John Foster, deceased, liberty is accordingly granted to him for the same by this Court, and none may presume to sett vp any other presse w[th]out the like liberty first granted.[1]

To the General Court, the monopoly feature of this concession was of course a measure of safety for the commonwealth, while to Mr. Sewall it was a privilege of some little commercial value. He continued in charge of the Boston press until September, 1684, when his retirement was provided for in these words : —

> Whereas, at a sessions of the Gennerall Court in October, 1681, this Court was pleased to intrust M[r] Samuel Sewall wth the mannagem[t] of the printing press in Boston, lately vnder the improovement of M[r] John Foster, deceased, and whereas, by the prouidence of God, M[r] Seawall is rendered vnable to attend the same, he judging it reasonable to acquaint this honnoured Court therewith,

[1] *Massachusetts Records,* v. 323–324; *Sewall Papers,* i. 57 ; *Massachusetts Archives,* lviii. 114.

desiring that he may be freed from any obligation
vnto duty respecting that affajre, wth thankfull
acknouledgm^{t}s of the liberty then granted, —
    The Court grants the request aboue mentioned.[1]

The monopoly which Mr. Sewall had resigned, having
been given to no one else, the printers whom he had employed continued their work under the supervision of the
regular licensers.[2] One of these printers, Samuel Green,
Jr., endeavored in 1685 to obtain for himself the coveted
monopoly, as is shown in the following petition : —

To the hono^{rable} Gen^{r}all Court, now Assembled
together in Boston, the humble petition of Sam^{ll}
Green printer
    Humbly sheweth to yor hono^{r}s
    That whereas Mr Sam^{ll} Seawall was ready &
willing for the publique good to vndertake the
manadgem^t of the printing press, And in Order
thereto for his better Incouragem^t the honord
Generall Court vpon the 12th of October In the
yeare of our Lord 1681 did see meete to Confirm
vnto him the whole priviledge thereof, & withall
did Order that none might set vp any other press
in Boston without the like Libertie. (Now may it
please yor hono^{rs}) seeing God by his providence
hath so ordered it to call vnto himselfe Capt John
Hull the honord father in Law of m^r Sam^{ll} Seawall, And since wch time, ye fores^d m^r Seawall is
called into A place of publique trust & other Con-
cerns, so y^t he cannot prosecute his designe as to
the printing worke. yor humble petition^r in obedi-

---

[1] *Massachusetts Records,* v. 452; *Sewall Papers,* i. 57; *Massachusetts
Archives,* lviii. 132.

[2] As in the earlier case of John Foster, no authorization allowing these
printers — Samuel Green, Jr., and Richard Pierce — to go on with their business can be found; but evidence that they continued to work is given by Green
and Paine in their papers on " Early American Imprints," under the years 1684,
1685, 1686. See Massachusetts Historical Society, *Proceedings,* February,
1895, pp. 459–472; American Antiquarian Society, *Proceedings,* October, 1895,
pp. 312–316.

ence to his hono^rd father Left his habitation, where
he then was. Being in New London in the Coloney of Conecticutt, And then in A Convenient
way of trading, wch by Gods blessing he was in
A very Comfortable way of Liueing, yet was willing & ready as well for the publique good as his
owne Interest And did remove himselfe & familie
out of the foresaid Coloney to Boston, since w^ch
time he hath been Assisting to the above s^d m^r
Seawall: Allso since the fores^d m^r Seawall haith
Left off the Improvm^t of the printing press, yor
humble petition^r hath Layd out Large sums of
money In purchaseing of seuerall Instrum̃^ts &
tools for the further Improving & promoting of
printing, whereby he hath straitned himselfe &
familie, hopeing thereby to attaine to the same
encouragem̃^t, libertie & lisence, wch is granted to
m^r Seawall. I humbly request yor hono^rs to take
it into yor serious Consideration, that I am a poore
man. And that I haue seuerall young children.
And the greatest part of ye Estate that I haue is
Layd out in tools & Instrum̃^ts as abovesaid, And
since yor poore petition^r did enter vpon the worke
of printing, which is about twentie yeares agoe,
And he having no other Calling to betake himselfe
vnto, whereby he may maintaine himselfe & familie, so hopeing this hon^rd Generall Court vpon
their prudent consideratiõ of the p^rmisses, will
see just cause to grant yor humble supplycant his
request herein which will be for the promotion of
the publque good as well as my benefitt In w^ch
worke I hope your hono^rs shall find him readier
in doeing then saying, to the vttermost of his
skill, In case yor hono^rs will be pleased to grant
yor humble petitio^r A Lesence & Confirme it
with as Large liberties for printing, As yor hono^rs
did to m^r Seawall, All wch being done by the
honord Generall Court for yor petition^r shall
engage, And as in dutie he is bound, for the con-
tinvance of yor hono^rs Long life with prosperitie
& Everlasting happines euer shall pray, so he is

yor hono^rs humble supplycant in all dutifull submission, And yor most humble servant

Samll: Green

Boston the 7th of May 1685 [1]

It is perhaps not remarkable that no action upon this
petition was taken. The colony charter had by this time
been vacated; and so unimportant a matter as the question of a monopoly of printing in Boston would attract
little attention in the midst of great public anxiety, at a
time when all measures of government were known to be
but temporary. Besides, the system of control of the
press by the official licensers was still unimpaired; the
plan had worked with such admirable smoothness that no
cases of disturbance of the public peace by seditious publications are recorded for a period of twenty years. The
power of the press being in the hands of leading men in
the commonwealth, their control was not likely to cause
any considerable friction till there should be a sharper
division on partisan lines.[2] Before the abrogation of the
charter, therefore, and the institution of a government not
of their own choosing, the people of Massachusetts as a
whole could not feel any serious deprivation in restrictions
upon the freedom of the press.

---

[1] *Massachusetts Archives,* lviii. 135.

[2] The status of the press in Pennsylvania, the only other colony having a
printer at this time, shows a similar condition there. William Bradford had
come to that province in 1685, with the approval of Penn and George Fox.
The first issue from his press was subjected to executive censorship, and he
was commanded to print nothing without license from the Council. His
frequent contests with governors, and with official meetings of Friends, quite
discouraged him, and in 1693 he left Pennsylvania. See *Pennsylvania
Records,* i, *passim ; Princeton Review,* i. 78 ff.

CHAPTER V.

LAX ENFORCEMENT OF CENSORSHIP, 1686–1716.

THE loss of the colony charter transferred the control of the press from the representatives of the people of Massachusetts to the appointed agents of the crown. Although the commission under which President Dudley acted as the executive head of the province from May to December, 1686, was but a temporary expedient of government, its ample powers were sufficient to authorize direction of the press. Parliamentary enactments for censorship continued to lend sanction to such a policy;[1] while Stuart theories of the prerogative maintained that the viceregal functions of the executive head of a royal province were quite extensive enough to warrant a control still broadly enforced by the crown in the mother country.[2] In 1684, when Charles II was planning to send out Colonel Kirke as "his Majesty's Lieutenant and Governor-General," it was resolved to insert in his instructions the clause "that nothing be printed in New England without the allowance of the Governor";[3] but the death of Charles and the ac-

[1] The interval of purely executive control of the press, which began in 1679, came to an end in 1685, when former licensing acts were revived by 1 James II, c. 17.

[2] On the powers of governors, see Greene, *The Provincial Governor in the English Colonies of North America;* see also ch. vi. below.

[3] Palfrey, *New England,* iii. 395, note, quoting from *Colonial Papers.* Another example of the same policy was given in the instructions to Lord Effingham, who was appointed governor of Virginia in 1683. He was ordered "to allow no person to use a printing press on any occasion whatsoever" (Thomas, *History of Printing,* i. 332). This was after the Virginia council had forbidden the printing of anything until the king's pleasure should be known (see Hening, *Statutes,* ii. 518).

cession of James II delayed the settlement of the colonial government, and Joseph Dudley was without specific instructions to regulate printing. Nevertheless, the unpopularity of the new government made the exercise of this power seem a necessity for the prevention of factious disorders, and to meet the need Secretary Randolph appears to have acted as licenser of the press. A new step was taken in the appointment of an official printer "to the Honorable his Majesties President and Council of this Government"; and Richard Pierce, one of Samuel Sewall's former employees, was elected to that position.[1] Evidence of the control actually exercised is seen in the following notification : —

> M.ʳ Greene.
> I am comanded by M.ʳ Secretary Randolph, to give you notice that you doe not proceed to print any Almanack whatever without haveing his approbation for yᵉ same.
> Yoʳˢ Ben : Bullivant

> Boston : 29 Novembʳ 1686[2]

In December, 1686, Edmund Andros arrived in Boston to assume his office as governor of New England; and it was quite in accord with the nature of his commission that a clause in his instructions should require him to control the press. In fact, it was now the established policy of the English government to give the "power of the press" to all provincial governors;[3] and for about

---

[1] "M.ʳ Pierce the Printers Petition received & referred to M.ʳ Secr.ʸ & M.ʳ Winthrop to do in it according as they shall see meet" (*Council Records*, ii. 84, October 27, 1686).

[2] *Mather Papers* (MSS.), vi. 28; printed in Massachusetts Historical Society, *Collections*, 4th series, viii. 663. Bullivant was attorney-general.

[3] Compare the instructions of Governor Dongan of New York, 1686, *New York Colonial Documents*, iii. 375 ; of Governor Copley of Maryland, 1691, *Maryland Archives*, viii. 279 ; of Lord Cornbury of New Jersey, 1702,

forty years the following paragraph appeared in their instructions : —

> And forasmuch as great inconvenience may arise by the liberty of printing within our said territory under your government you are to provide by all necessary orders that no person keep any printing-press for printing, nor that any book pamphlet or other matters whatsoever be printed without your especial leave and license first obtained.[1]

A few weeks after the installation of his government, Governor Andros took steps to put into effect this important article of his instructions. The proceedings of his Council contain this entry : —

MINUTES.

Thursday the 28th of January 1686.

> The Councill being met His Ex[ce] acquainted them that it was his Maj[ties] express commands that the printing Presses in the Towns of Boston and Cambridge in New England should be effectuall taken care of. Upon which an order passed

---

New Jersey Archives, ii. 534 ; of Governor Hunter of New York, 1709, *New York Colonial Documents,* v. 142. Such instructions would but make colonial practice conform to English precedent, as long as licensing continued in the mother country. For the inconsistency which arose after 1695, see below, pp. 77–78.

[1] Quoted in Massachusetts Historical Society, *Proceedings,* June, 1893, p. 273, by Mr. A. C. Goodell, "by permission of The Colonial Society of Massachusetts, from the second volume of their publications, now in press." This volume consists of commissions and instructions to Massachusetts governors. By the kindness of Mr. Goodell, the author was permitted to examine manuscript copies of instructions to all the governors who were directed to control the press.

The clause in the instructions of Governor Andros, quoted above, is taken from the first set given to him in 1686. When, in 1688, his jurisdiction was extended over New York and New Jersey, the article was again put into his instructions. See *Rhode Island Records,* iii. 253–254 ; *New York Colonial Documents,* iii. 548.

F

in Councill, that no Papers, Bookes Pamphlets &c should be printed in New England untill Licensed according to Law, and that no printer have Liberty to print till he hath given five hundred pounds security to his Maj[tie] to observe that order.[1]

The terms of the order were as follows : —

That Coppyes of books &c[a] to be printed be first p[r]used by m[r] Dudley late President & vpon his allowance of them for the pres that one Coppy thereof So allowed and attested by him be brought to y[e] Secr[y] office. to be left on record and receave from him an Imprimatur.[2]

When a policy that had been thought a necessary precaution for orderly government was now turned against the old local leaders by the governor, the people of Massachusetts were in a position to feel that restraints upon the freedom of the press were a grievance. Byfield, in his "Account of the Revolution in New England," said that Andros "would neither suffer them [the laws] to be printed nor fairly published."[3] The author of "An Appeal to the Men of New England" complained because "the late wise Justices . . . so vigorously prosecuted that worthy minister Mr. Mather the Younger for publishing (before Sir Edmond Andros arrived here) a modest and placid discourse giving the reasons of our Dissent from the ceremonies of the Church of England." He asked " of what value with them was the late Kings Declaration for Liberty of Conscience?" and whether, "when they had the power of binding and loosing the PRESS, it had not

---

[1] *Council Records*, ii. III.

[2] *Massachusetts Archives*, cxxvi. 224 ; printed in Massachusetts Historical Society, *Collections*, 3d series, vii. 171.   John Tully's almanacs for 1688 and 1689, printed in Boston by Samuel Green, have upon the title-pages, " Imprimatur Edm. Randolph. Secr." See *New England Historical and Genealogical Register*, viii. 21.

[3] *Andros Tracts*, i. 14, marginal note.

been more satisfactory for them to have answered it by
Scripture and reason, or any way rather than by a ruinous
Romish Persecution."[1] So, too, when John Winslow
brought to New England "a Treasonable Paper" containing the news that William of Orange had taken the
field against James II, Andros endeavored to suppress
the paper and imprisoned its unlucky bearer.[2] Finally, an
official apology of Andros for the course of his government, made to prove that he had faithfully attempted to
carry out his instructions, recited that "order was taken
that nothing should be printed without license."[3]

The overthrow of the Andros government in April, 1689,
followed by the resumption of authority under the forms
of the colony charter,[4] again put the control of printing
into the hands of the General Court. It soon became evident, however, that there had been no conversion to a
belief in freedom of the press. "Disorderly printing"
may not have been uncommon in the first months of un-
settled government; for in November the House of Representatives issued this severe warning against all such
disturbances of the public peace : —

> Whereas many papers haue beene lately printed
> & dispersed tending to the disturbance of the peace
> & subuersion of the gouermt of this theire Maies-
> ties Collonie King William & Queene Mary It is
> therfor ordered that if any person or persons
> within this Collony be found guilty of any such

---

[1] *Andros Tracts*, iii. 200.   [2] *Ibid.* i. 77–79.

[3] The interesting paper from which this item is quoted is in the London
Public Record Office, *Colonial Papers, America and West Indies*, i. 397–410.
It is entitled, "Answer of Sir Edmond Andros to his Instructions," and is
arranged in parallel columns, in one of which the writer gives his instructions
(dated Whitehall, April 16, 1688), and in the other makes comments showing
his difficulties or his success in carrying out the many specifications.

[4] The story of the revolution and of the setting up of temporary government is told in Palfrey, *New England,* iii. 579–589, and in Barry, *Massachusetts,*
i. 502-510.

like Misdemeanour of printing publishing or concealing any such like papers or discourses or not
timely discouer such things to Authority or doe
any act or thing that tends to the disturbance of
the peace or the subuersion of this gouermt —
They shall be accounted enemies to theire Maies-
ties present Gouermt & be proceeded ag^t as such
with uttermost Seuerity

   Past in the affirmative by the Representatives
        Ebenezer Prout Clerk
Nov^{br} 8th : 1689 [1]

When the government found it necessary to enlighten
the people on the course of public affairs, it authorized
Samuel Green to publish a broadside entitled " The Present State of the New-English Affairs," and bearing the
indorsement " This is Published to prevent False Reports." The paper was made up of extracts from the
letters of Increase Mather, the colony's agent in London,
and from the London *Publick News-Letter*, together with
the orders lately received from the king to send the imprisoned members of the Andros government to England
for trial.[2]

On September 25, 1690, the community was startled by
the appearance of an unlicensed news-sheet, bearing the
title *Publick Occurrances, both Foreign and Domestick*. It
was printed at Boston by Richard Pierce for Benjamin
Harris, and is well known as the first newspaper printed
within the limits of what is now the United States.[3] The

---

[1] *Massachusetts Archives*, xxxv. 77–78; printed in *Andros Tracts*, iii. 107.
Pennsylvania was still the only other colony having a printing-press. Bradford
again suffered prosecution this year, being put under bonds not to print any-
thing without Governor Blackwell's license. The governor claimed that " the
Proprietor had declared himselfe against the using of the printing presse."
See *Pennsylvania Records*, i. 278; *Princeton Review*, i. 85.

[2] An original copy of the broadside is in *Massachusetts Archives*, xxxv. 83;
a reprint is in New Hampshire Historical Society, *Collections* (1866), viii.
458–460. It had none of the attributes of a newspaper.

[3] For notices of this first American newspaper, see *Sewall Papers*, i. 332

project of the ambitious publisher was nipped in the bud; for the Governor and Council soon issued a broadside declaring their "high resentment and disallowance" of the said pamphlet, and strictly forbidding any person "for the future to set forth anything in print without license first obtained." [1]

When the province charter went into operation in 1692, the control of the press again passed into the hands of the royal governors, the instructions to Andros on this point being repeated in almost identical phraseology to each governor until 1730. [2] Governor Phips was too much a creature of the Mathers, however, to cause any trouble over the control of public discussion, except in so far as there should be rebellion against the dominating influence of these worthies. In May, 1692, the business of printing in Massachusetts was still confined to Cambridge and Boston. In the university town, Samuel Green, Sr., and his son Bartholomew were in charge of the only press, [3] while

---

("Sept. 25. A printed sheet entituled publick Occurrences comes out, which gives much distaste because not Licensed; and because of the passage referring to the French King and the Maquas"); Hudson, *American Journalism*, 44–48; Winsor, *Memorial History of Boston*, ii. 387, and *Narrative and Critical History*, v. 90; North, *The Newspaper and Periodical Press* (United States *Tenth Census*, viii), 10–11; *Magazine of American History*, xvii. 3. The paper was reprinted in the *Historical Magazine* for August, 1857.

[1] A copy of the broadside is in the library of the Massachusetts Historical Society, and it is printed in the *Proceedings* of the society for December, 1892. Tully's almanacs for 1690 and 1691 do not bear an imprimatur; neither does Newman's *Harvard's Ephemeris* for 1690 (see Harvard University Library, shelf number 14378.4, and *New England Historical and Genealogical Register*, viii. 21).

[2] See A. C. Goodell, in Massachusetts Historical Society, *Proceedings*, June, 1893, p. 273.

[3] Samuel Green, Jr., had died in July, 1690, and Bartholomew Green's office had been burned in September of the same year. See *Massachusetts Archives*, lviii. 137–139 (papers comprising bills for printing by Samuel Green from April 26, 1689, to July 26, 1690, by Samuel Green's executor to August 25, 1690, and by Bartholomew Green from April 20 to October 27, 1691).

Richard Pierce was conducting what was probably the sole printing establishment in Boston. Benjamin Harris was still a Boston bookseller and a patron of the printers. To him, on December 16, 1692, Governor Phips gave an order allowing him to publish the "Acts and Laws";[1] and on June 6, 1693, Bartholomew Green, wishing to set up a new printing-office in Boston, obtained the requisite permission from the Governor and Council by the following vote: —

> Barthô Green, Printer, is allowed to Set up his Press and exercise his Trade within the Town of Boston for the Printing of what shall be duely Licensed, and Nothing else
>
> William Phips[2]

Thus far the province government had been concerned with the maintenance of restrictive censorship. A different sort of contest for the control of the press arose when Thomas Maule, a Salem Quaker, was arraigned as the first person in the province to be prosecuted for the crime of libel. Maule had been in trouble as early as 1669, when he was sentenced to receive ten stripes for saying that Mr. Higginson "preached lies, and that his instruction was the doctrine of devils." His own account of his many troubles states that he was five times imprisoned, thrice deprived of his goods, and thrice whipped. Now, in 1695, he wished to publish a book exploiting his theological opinions, and sent his manuscript to New York to be printed,

---

[1] Buckingham, *Reminiscences*, i. 3.

[2] *General Court Records* (Mss.), vi. 283; see also Thomas, *History of Printing*, i. 89–90. New York, instead of Pennsylvania, now became the only other one of the colonies that had a press. William Bradford left Philadelphia for New York early in 1693, because of the ruinous restraints to which he had been subjected by church and state. Yet his status in his new location was merely that of a government printer, and he could print nothing without license. See *New York Colonial Documents*, iv–v, *passim; New York Historical Manuscripts, passim; New York Laws, passim.*

because he was able to get a license to publish it from the governor of that province. The importation and circulation of this book in Massachusetts brought upon him a prompt prosecution. On December 12, 1695, the Council took action as follows : —

Upon perusal of a printed Pamphlet Entituled Truth held forth, and Maintained, put forth in the Name of Thomas Maule, said to be Thomas Maule of Salem, containing many Notorious, and Wicked Lies, and Slanders not only on private persons, but upon Governm^t, and also divers Corrupt, and pernicious Doctrines, utterly, Subversive of the True Christian, and professed Faith

Ordered

That a Warrant be made out unto the Sheriff of Essex or his Deputy forthwith to Search the House of Thomas Maul of Salem, and other places, where he may be informed any of the said Books are, And to Seize and Secure the same And also to cause the said Maul to Appear before the Lieut Governour, and Council on Thursday the 19th Currant, at the Council Chamber to Answer what shall be Objected against him on his Majesties behalf in the Premises, As also that a Warrant be made out to Search all Booksellers Shops, where any of the Said Pamphlets are or may be exposed to sale, And to Secure the same

William Stoughton [1]

Two days later the House of Representatives expressed its sentiments in the following vote : —

Whereas there is lately printed & published a Pamphlet in Quarto containing Two hundred & Sixty Pages, entitled *Truth held forth & maintained* &c. *by Thomas Maule printed in the year 1695.* Which is stuff'd with many notorious and pernicious Lies and Scandals, not only against particular & privat persons; but also against the

[1] *General Court Records,* vi. 436.

Government Churches and Ministry; and against those Worthies who first followed Christ into these uttermost Ends of the Earth, as if they had therein loosed themselvs from His Yoke, & shaken off his Burden: As also many corrupt Expressions in point of Doctrine, perverting the Scriptures, and subverting the True Christian Religion

The Representatives of this His Majesties Province humbly pray, that the premisses may be enquired into, and some suitable Testimony born against the Author and his Evil work.

Dec: 14th: 1695 Read & Voted in the house of Representatiues & past in the Affirmatiue & sent up to the honble Lt Gour. & Councill for a Concurrance

Nehemiah Jewett. Speaker.[1]

Maule made his appearance before the Council on December 19, with " his Bible under his arm," as Sewall says, " expecting to be examined in some point of religion." [2] The records tell the story of the examination as follows: —

Thomas Maule of Salem being convented before the Board for putting forth a Printed Pamphlett or Booke Entituled: Truth held forth and maintained, containing many notorious & wicked lyes & scandals not only upon private persons, but also upon Governt & likewise divers corrupt & pernicious Doctrines utterly subversive of the true Christian & professed faith &ca

The sd Maule owned the Booke to be his, and that he wrote it, except the errors committed by the Printer.

Ordered: That the sd Bookes now under seizure both at Boston and Salem be publickly burnt here and there, and that sd Thomas Maule give Bond of two hundred pounds himselfe & one hundred pounds apiece two sureties for the said Maules appearance at the next Court of Assize & General Goale Delivery, to be holden within the

---

[1] *Massachusetts Archives*, xi. 101.   [2] *Sewall Papers*, i. 416.

County of Essex to answer what shall be objected ag[st] him on his Maj[tys] behalfe for being the Author of said Booke.

W[m] Stoughton.[1]

For some reason no indictment was found against him at the Ipswich session of the Superior Court of Judicature ; but, after he had cited Matthew xxvii. 7, and Acts i. 18, in open court, to prove that there were as great mistakes in the Bible as any in his book,[2] he was bound over to the November session to be held in Salem. The indictment returned in November contained two counts, one covering the offence of publishing his book, the other his denial of Scripture inerrancy. His trial was a triumph of shrewd reliance upon the current reaction against the credulity of the witchcraft prosecutions. By adroitly pleading that the printed book was no more to be received as good evidence of his guilt than " the spectre evidence is in law sufficient to prove a person accused by such evidence to be a witch," he played upon the prejudices of the jury, and won an acquittal in the first criminal trial in Massachusetts for a printed libel.[3]

[1] *Council Records*, ii. 372 (December 19, 1695).

[2] For the recognizance of Thomas Maule to appear at Ipswich, see *Suffolk Court Files* (Mss.), No. 3327a(1). His sureties were Thomas Bannister and Robert Calef. The bond is dated December 20, 1695, and is signed by "Sam Sewall." The record of the action at the Ipswich court is in *Records of Superior Court of Judicature* (Mss.), 1695–1700, p. 72. *Suffolk Court Files*, No. 3327a(2), is a memorandum showing that on the third Tuesday in May, 1696, Maule declared in open court at Ipswich his belief that there were as great mistakes in the Bible as any in his book.

[3] The record of the trial and acquittal is in *Records of Superior Court of Judicature*, 1695–1700, p. 80. Sewall notices the result in these words : "Grand jury present Tho Maule for publishing his scandalous Book. Jury of Tryals, of whom Capt Turner and Capt. King were two, bring him in Not Guilty, at which he Triumphs. Mr. Bullivant spake for him, but modestly and with respect" (*Sewall Papers*, i. 436). The triumphant Quaker again got into print in 1697, when he published his *New England Persecutors Mauled with their own Weapons*. Some additional notices of his troubles

An excellent illustration of the status of the Boston press at the opening of the eighteenth century is furnished by the controversy that arose out of the establishment of a new church in Boston, in 1699, with Benjamin Colman as pastor. As the principles of this congregation varied in a number of points from the forms of church government and public worship prescribed by the Cambridge Platform and followed by the older Boston churches, they promptly excited suspicion, which was met by a " Manifesto, or Declaration, set forth by the Undertakers of the New Church." This notice, however, not only failed to remove the prejudices of those who suspected covert Presbyterianism or Episcopacy, but even aroused more outspoken opposition. Under the inspiration of the Mathers, the leaders of the movement were stigmatized as "innovators, . . . ignorant, arrogant, obstinate," and dangerous to the peace of the province. The efforts of Lieutenant-Governor Stoughton, Chief-Justice Sewall, Reverend Samuel Willard, and others finally availed to patch up a truce between the heated partisans; but the reconciliation was only temporary. It had been hard enough to submit to the maintenance of the Episcopal worship under the patronage of royal officials resident in the colony; but the Mathers could not remain quiet and allow the strength of the old exclusive position to be sapped by even passive acquiescence in the errors of men who claimed to be part of the same household of faith. In March, 1700, Increase Mather published a treatise entitled *The Gospel Order Professed and Practiced by the Churches of Christ in New England Justified*, which he designed to be an antidote to the infection of the new church. An answer was prepared by the Reverend Mr. Colman and his friends, with the title *Gospel Order Revived*. Since the authors were unwilling to sub-

are found in Chandler, *Criminal Trials*, i. 141–149; A. C. Goodell, in Essex Institute, *Historical Collections*, iii. 250–251; Winsor, *Narrative and Critical History*, v. 95.

mit the manuscript to the lieutenant-governor, and since the printer, Bartholomew Green, who was a member of the Old South Church, would not publish it without an imprimatur, it was sent to New York to be printed.

When copies of the pamphlet arrived in Boston, Green found himself an object of notice; for they contained the following "Advertisement": "The *Reader* is desired to take Notice, that the Press in *Boston* is so much under the aw of the Reverend Author, whom we answer, and his Friends, that we could not obtain of the Printer there to print the following Sheets, which is the only true Reason why we have sent the Copy so far for its Impression and where it [is] printed with some Difficulty." The printer was quick to repudiate the charge, pleading that he had simply done his duty in refusing to print a work of controversy without official permission, and reciting cases to show the practice in such matters. " Nor was it a new thing," he announced in a handbill, " to shew Copies to the Lieutenant Governour in order to their being Printed. Mr. *Sewall's Phænomena Apocalyptica* was taken off the Press, and carried to the Lieutenant Governour for his Allowance. By the same Token, one Half Sheet being wrought off too soon: the Author was at the Charge to Print it over again, to gratify His Honour in some Alterations that could not otherwise be made. Besides other Instances that might be given." Green was cautious because of previous experience; for he said in his deposition: "It came into my mind what great disturbance the Manifesto had made (which I Printed very privately at said Tuthill's desire) which made me the more thoughtful, lest this might give more Offence." Yet he admits having published some things without license, and his opponents point out that Mr. Mather's book was not licensed.[1]

[1] For an account of the "Manifesto" referred to by Green, and of the controversy to which it was incidental, see *New England Historical and*

It is plain that custom was working the decay of censorship when manuscripts were thus submitted to a licenser only in special cases, because printers or publishers did not dare risk punishment for presuming to print without "license first obtained." If authors were in favor with the government, or did not indulge in controversy, a license might safely be dispensed with, although official form still required the imprimatur.[1]

While the exercise of censorship over occasional pamphlets was neglected, a different policy persisted with regard to the appearance of periodicals devoted to the publication of general news. It was now some fourteen years since the first attempt to establish a newspaper in Boston had resulted in the prompt suppression of Harris's unauthorized *Publick Occurrances*. Since then, either manuscript news-letters or uncertain supplies of papers from England had been the only resource of those who wished to keep themselves informed of the news of the world. Postmaster Campbell had for some time been using the advantages of his position in Boston to establish a business as news-letter writer for regular patrons.[2] The greater prac-

---

Genealogical Register, iii. 116–117, 220–212. Copies of Increase Mather's book, of the *Gospel Order Revived*, and of the handbills issued on both sides are in the library of the Massachusetts Historical Society. Reprints of the handbills are in Thomas, *History of Printing*, i. 415–423.

[1] Robert Calef's *More Wonders of the Invisible World* was another book causing trouble in Boston in 1700. Dr. Eliot (*Biographical Dictionary*, 95) says that Increase Mather caused the "wicked book to be burned in the College yard." Cotton Mather was very angry over the charges which it made against his father and himself. The book also had its place in the religious and partisan quarrels between the Mathers and their opponents. Calef argued against spectral evidence in witchcraft trials. See Poole on "Witchcraft in Boston," in Winsor, *Memorial History of Boston*, ii. 165–172.

[2] The work of John Campbell, the new postmaster of New England, as a writer of news-letters is illustrated by a number of his epistles to Governor Fitz-John Winthrop, from April 12, to October, 1703, printed in Massachusetts Historical Society, *Proceedings*, March, 1867, pp. 485–501.

tical convenience of printed news-sheets must have been obvious, especially in view of the well-known rapid development and popularity of newspapers in England.[1] The government of William and Mary had at first continued to administer the licensing system as developed under the Stuarts, and in 1693 extended the statute of 1685 for two years.[2] The blunders of inefficient licensers caused great irritation and were the occasion for some significant protests against these restraints upon the press;[3] and the influence of more liberal principles in politics, added to an increasing recognition of the utility of newspapers, prepared the way for an abandonment of censorship. Although the House of Lords voted, in 1695, to continue the old system, the Commons refused to acquiesce; and the Lords yielded without a contest. The arguments which carried the day for liberality were not those of Milton's "Areopagitica,"—pleas for the broadest liberty of thought and discussion. Instead, the opponents of licensing relied chiefly upon an exposition of the inconveniences and absurdities of the statute which was about to expire, John Locke giving great service in this direction.[4] Probably most conservative men expected that Parliament would soon pass some statute to regulate the press which would be effective and yet would avoid the absurdities of the obsolete system; and, indeed, the House of Lords annually passed such measures for the next four years, but the bills were consistently rejected by the Commons.[5] The administration dominated by William III was not

[1] On the rise of English newspapers after the expiration of the licensing act in 1695, see Bourne, *English Newspapers*, i. ch. iii.

[2] 4 William & Mary, c. 24.

[3] Macaulay, *England*, ch. xix.

[4] The eighteen reasons offered on the part of the Commons in conference on the licensing act are given in *Commons Journals*, xi. 305–306. For Locke's part in the discussion, see Bourne, *Locke*, ii. 312–316.

[5] See *Commons Journals*, xi–xii, *passim*.

disposed to attempt to continue censorship under the doctrine of royal prerogative which had prevailed from 1679 to 1685; so that this form of restriction upon the freedom of the English press was finally abandoned.

The peculiarity of conditions in Massachusetts, as a royal province under a governor whose instructions required him to maintain the licensing system, permitted the continuance of a degree of control no longer possible in the mother country. Therefore the *News-Letter*, appearing in Boston on April 24, 1704, and noteworthy as the first regular newspaper in America, bore the announcement that it was "published by authority."[1] In the enterprise of substituting a printed paper for his manuscript news-letters, Postmaster Campbell had the encouragement and assistance of the government;[2] and he, on his part, ad-

---

[1] The *News-Letter* has been noticed and described many times. See *Magazine of American History*, xvii. 3; *Historical Magazine*, December, 1865, p. 368; Thomas, *History of Printing*, ii. 12 ff.; Wheildon, *Curiosities of History*, 86–97 (containing a facsimile of an issue of the *News-Letter*). The author has consulted the files preserved in the libraries of the Massachusetts Historical Society and the American Antiquarian Society, and in the Lenox Library.

[2] In 1703 and 1704, Campbell petitioned for allowances from the public treasury of Massachusetts, which were granted him; and in April and October, 1706, also, money for his services to the public was voted him. The status of his paper is revealed by certain paragraphs in his petitions: —

"Your Petitioner also having Last year sett on foott, a weekly Letter of Intelligence for both foreign and Domestick occurrences, expecting that the Incomes thereby being sett at a Moderate Rate, would be sufficient to defraÿ the Necessarÿ Charge thereof; The which it did not do, And this year several Gentlemen, Merchants and others being willing it should not drop, but be continued, haue Agreed to contribute towards It's support for an other year: yet Notwithstanding there are not a Competent number that offers to carry it on, And It being found beneficial & of Publick use and service to the Countreÿ to prevent a great manÿ false reports" (*Massachusetts Acts and Resolves*, viii. 562–563).

"And That ÿour Petitioner for a Publick Good above Two ÿears ago has been at the Cost and Charge to print a weeklÿ Letter of Intelligence of both fforeign and Domestick Occurrences, which was sett at a More Moderat

hered closely to the policy of avoiding all offence to the government. This peaceful conservatism characterized the management of the *News-Letter* for the period of more than fifteen years during which Mr. Campbell continued to publish it as the only newspaper in Massachusetts.

The administration of Governor Dudley, extending from 1702 to 1716, led to an unusual development of partisanship, and to the first considerable use of the press in Massachusetts for political warfare. The columns of the *News-Letter* were not open for such discussions; but controversial pamphlets were numerous,[1] and appeared without licenses, a fact which shows that Governor Dudley did not maintain the control enjoined by his instructions.[2]

price then it was in some part of England, notwithstanding the Charge here is above ffour times dearer then it would cost there, yet your Petitioner has not had sufficient Encouragement to defray the Necessarÿ Charge thereof" (*Massachusetts Acts and Resolves*, viii. 630).

[1] See a list of titles in Thomas, *History of Printing*, ii. 349–376. Public censure in one case was voted by the General Court on December 5, 1705, in these terms : —

"In Council.

" Ordered.

"That two Irreligious prophane & scandalous printed Pamphlets sent to this Court, with a Letter Subscribed John Rogers & John Rogers, jun. be burn'd in the great Street in Boston neer the whipping Post, by the Common Execution^r, on the morrow at one oclock afternoon.

" Js. Addington, Secry.

" Sent down for Concurrence.

" In the House of Representatives.

" Die pdict. Read & Pass'd a Concurrence.

"Thomas Oakes, Speak^r.

" Consent to

" J. Dudley." — *Massachusetts Archives*, lviii. 244.

Another instance of official book burning was recorded in April, 1712. John Green, of Boston, mariner or schoolmaster, was fined five pounds and put under bonds for publishing "a most prophane, filthy & obscene discourse or mock sermon, tending to vilify the word & ordinances of God, & to debauch & corrupt the morals of the youth of this place." Furthermore, "the original book & the copies thereof" were ordered to be publicly burned by the common hangman. See *Records of General Sessions of the Peace*, i. 246–247.

[2] During the years of Governor Dudley's administration in Massachusetts

During the uncertain days of 1715, between the expiration of his commission by limitation and the receipt of an order temporarily reinstating him, his opponents even took advantage of the situation to suppress a statement published by his son Paul Dudley to vindicate his father. The five printers of the colony — Bartholomew Green, James Cummins, Thomas Fleet, Nicholas Boone, and John Allen — were personally examined by the Council, in the effort to discover the author of "A printed Sheet . . . entituled the Case of His Excellency the Gov.ʳ & Council of the Province of the Massachusetts Bay in New England, truly stated." Thomas Fleet was with difficulty induced to admit that he had secretly printed the disquieting paper for Mr. Samuel Tyley. Mr. Tyley was then sent for, and acknowledged that he had been the agent of Paul Dudley to get the printing done. Finally, the Council ordered the sheriff to seize all copies of the paper, and issued a declaration to negative its influence.[1]

The following year, after Governor Dudley had definitively retired from his office, the Council, under control of his political opponents, dealt in a similar manner with a broadside published by his son-in-law, William Dummer. This paper consisted of an abstract of an article on Massachusetts politics from the London *Flying Post*. As soon as the Council was informed of the publication and had

censorship was still enforced in New York by Governors Cornbury and Hunter (see *New York Historical Manuscripts*, lii. 129; *New York Colonial Documents*, v. 205). Of the other colonies, only Pennsylvania, Connecticut, and Rhode Island had any printing-presses as yet. Pennsylvania, having had a press under the strict control of a committee of Friends until 1712, saw a revival of printing by Andrew Bradford in that year. Connecticut and Rhode Island had official public printers during part of the period. Just what was the status of the business of Thomas Short and Timothy Green in New London, and of Andrew Bradford in Newport and Philadelphia, the contemporary records in print do not enable one to say. See Thomas, *History of Printing*, *passim*.

[1] *Council Records*, vi. 330–332 (March 16–18, 1714–15).

listened to the reading of its contents, it passed a vote forbidding Mr. Dummer to distribute the broadside and summoning him and certain of his friends for examination. The printer of the paper testified that he had printed it for Mr. Dummer, a fact which the latter gentleman readily admitted. Thereupon, as the official proceedings record :—

> The Question being put whether M^r. William Dummers ordering the reprinting & dispersing a paper Intituled "An Abstract from the Flying Post or the Post Master from Saturday March 23rd. to Tuesday March 6th. 1715/16 which contains certain votes of the General Court with reflections accompanying the same does not highly tend to the disservice of His Majesty and the disturbance & disquiet of His Majestys Good Subjects of this Province
>
> Voted in the affirmative . . .
>
> Ordered That M^r. William Dummer & M^r. Francis Wainwright be sent for to the Board that the Vote passed yesterday relating to M^r. Dummer be now read to him in Council, And that Samuel Sewall, Esqr. do reprimand him for his reprinting & dispersing a paper intituled an Abstract from the Flying Post or the Post Master from Saturday Mar: the 3rd. to Tuesday March the 6th. 1715/6 and that he admonish M^r. Dummer & M^r. Wainwright for the future not to intermeddle with the affairs of the Government [1]

Sewall, who although he believed in "upholding Government whether in or out of it," was friendly to Mr. Dummer, gives the following account of the scene before the Council :—

> Lt. Govr and Council order'd me to Reprimand Mr. Dummer. Having confronted the Lt Govr in his Favour, I finally was forc'd to do it. I told him how intolerable it was for privat persons to print Reflections and Censures on the highest

[1] *Council Records*, vi. 458–462 (May 26–29, 1716).

Acts of Government; To do it on one part was to do it on all; for they must be Together. Twas ill done of them who printed it in London, and twas ill done of them that carried it on here. Mr. Bromfield had inform'd that he treated him scurvily by saying, They do not treat him as a Gentleman to send for him so often. I took notice of that; said twas easier for men to Comit a fault, than to bear to be told of it; he had therein forgot his Breeding. About 190. [copies] were left with Mr. Dumer's wife by Fleet. Dumer said he knew not what was become of them, own'd he had seen the prints at his House. But it apear'd his Broʳ Wainwright dispers'd them after the Lᵗ Govʳ had vehemently forbid it. . . . It seem'd to be very ill design'd to throw us into confusion just at the Election.[1]

The significance of the whole affair for the present purpose lies in its revelation of the continued disregard of censorship in a time of political excitement, together with the maintenance by the Council, in 1716, of an unquestioned right summarily to suppress any printed matter that displeased it. The thoroughness and directness of executive government in Massachusetts, corresponding to the provincial simplicity of all social institutions, kept the community free from the characteristic complications of libel trials and " taxes on knowledge " which hampered the English press of the period.

[1] *Sewall Papers,* iii. 84–85.

CHAPTER VI.

LAST EFFORTS TO MAINTAIN CENSORSHIP, 1716–1723.

THE animated political controversies which characterized the administration of Governor Samuel Shute, beginning in 1716, were marked by important developments for the freedom of the press. Calamitous conditions as to trade and currency, says Hutchinson, prepared the minds of the people "for impressions from pamphlets, courants, and other news-papers which were frequently published." [1] The opposition, or "patriot," party utilized the press to conduct its agitation; and when the governor attempted to enforce his nominal prerogative as licenser, it simply declined to concede to him the advantage which would result from that power.

The issue was first clearly drawn at the May session of the General Court in 1719, by differences between the House and the Council over an impost bill. In that bill the House inserted a clause taxing imports of English goods, a step which the Council declared to be contrary to the will of the king as expressed in recent instructions to the governor. The House insisted upon its position, on the ground that the charter gave the legislature power to levy taxes, and that the imposition of reasonable tariffs did not come within the king's prohibition of acts injurious to British commerce. The dispute became acrimonious, and the controversy descended into useless recrimina-

[1] Hutchinson, *Massachusetts*, ii. 210.

tions.   After Governor Shute had intervened with a molli-
fying speech, the House was induced to pass the bill
without the clause taxing imports of English goods; but
the retreat was accompanied by an ungracious preamble,
in which the House expressed its dissatisfaction and
offended the Council by implied censure.   The Council
tried in vain to induce the House to refrain from printing
this obnoxious preamble, and then responded with a public
justification of its own course in following the royal instructions.   Since neither the Council nor the governor seems to
have questioned the right of the House to publish its proceedings, the incident ended in favor of the popular
branch.[1]

But Governor Shute and his Council did not abandon
their efforts to hold writers and publishers to the careful
handling of political and religious questions; for within a
few months they distinctly and successfully asserted their
power to prevent John Checkley from publishing a tract
entitled "The Religion of Jesus Christ the only True
Religion."   This pamphlet was to be a reprint of Leslie's
"Short and Easy Method with the Deists," with Checkley's
additions and comments, in which he, as a devoted Episcopalian, classed deists and dissenters in a common condemnation.   Upon the appearance of an advertisement
announcing the proposed publication, a formidable committee, made up of the Council and four ministers, was
appointed to investigate the matter; and meanwhile the
printers were directed not to proceed in the printing
until further order.   The committee examined the author

---

[1] *General Court Records*, x. 363, 364, 365, 368, 369, 377, 379–391 (*passim*),
392 (the obnoxious preamble), 393 (the Council asks the House not to print
the preamble), 394, 395; see also Hutchinson, *Massachusetts*, ii. 204–208.
There was a somewhat similar incident in New York in 1711.   There, however, Governor Hunter seized in the printing-house all the copies of a representation by the assembly and suppressed them.   See *New York Colonial
Documents*, v. 205.

without satisfactory results, and made the following report : —

In Obedience to an order of His Excellency the Gov.ʳ & Council of the 5.ᵗʰ of February inst.ᵗ referring to a Book & Treatise in the Press mentioned in an advertisem.ᵗ, We sent for Fleet the Printer, who acquaint.ᵈ us that he had printed about four sheets, which we found to be a Book formerly printed, entituled, A Short & easy Method with the Deists, & which we could have recom̄end.ᵈ for the design & substance of it ; And at the same time the Printer informed us, that M.ʳ John Checkley of Boston, Shop keeper was his imployer & had in manuscript the other part of the Book or Treatise, we sent for the s.ᵈ Checkley, with whom many arguments were used by the Committee to persuade him to withhold the s.ᵈ other part of his intended Treatise from the Press or at least to communicate it to the Committee for examination, but without the desired effect the s.ᵈ Checkley declining to do either, till he might be satisfied His Excellency the Governour had any authority or Instruction referring to the Press. On the 17.ᵗʰ the Committee mett again & sent for M.ʳ Checkley after having given him satisfaction as to His Excell.ᶜʸˢ Instructions relateing to the Press, the Committee labour.ᵈ to perswade him either to suppress his s.ᵈ Treatise & not proceed in the printing of it, or to communicate it to the Committee & refer it to their examination, at least allow his own Ministers the Rev.ᵈ M.ʳ Miles & M.ʳ Harris to peruse the same, but he absolutely refused to comply with any of the proposals before mentioned, alledging that he had promised never to shew his Treatise to any person whatsoever before he published it, and alltho' he promised not to print s.ᵈ Treatise here, in case it were forbidden by His Excellency, yet he would not oblige himself that it should not be printed elsewhere [1]

[1] *Council Records*, vii. 12–13 (February 18, 1718–19).

On the report of the committee, the Council passed this order, which Checkley obeyed : —

> His Excellency the Governor & the Council having taken into consideration the report of the Comittee relating to an advertisem[t] of a Book & Treatise in the Press & apprehending by the contents of the s[d] advertisem[t] as well as by other information that there may be matters contained in the s[d] Treatise that may disturb the Peace and good agreement among the Churches in this Province of all denominations & M[r] John Checkley of Boston the Author or Publisher thereof refusing to let His Excellency, the Committee appointed for that purpose & even his own Ministers, the Reverend M[r] Miles & M[r] Harris, have the perusal of his Manuscr[pt] before it be printed
>
> It is therefore ordered that this Treatise be not printed till further order from this Board [1]

The success which attended these proceedings against a humble champion of an unpopular agitation proved that it was still possible, in 1719, to invoke the almost obsolete power of censorship ; but the policy followed by Governors Bellomont, Dudley, and Shute for the past twenty years, when they tolerated in their provincial jurisdiction much the same sort of freedom of the press which prevailed then in England, could not fail to have its effect.   Later events in this same year furnished an occasion for a decisive test of a governor's prerogative in this matter.   Governor Shute's speech at the November session of the General Court contained a paragraph which seemingly charged the province with neglecting to coöperate for the proper conservation of forests as sources of naval supplies.[2]   The governor

---

[1] *Council Records*, vii. 13–14.

[2] A manuscript copy of the speech, delivered November 4, 1719, and containing the offensive paragraph as to the conservation of woods, is in *General Court Records*, x. 398–400. It was printed in the *News-Letter*, No. 812, November 9, 1719 (Lenox Library).

presented the matter because his instructions required it; but that fact did not soften the effect of the speech. The House was stung to anger, and drew up an " Answer," or " Remonstrance," in which the surveyor of the woods was charged with gross misconduct in office.[1] The governor championed the cause of the surveyor, and requested the House not to print the "Remonstrance" in its votes, declaring that it was not a proper answer to his speech, and that it was not for his honor and the service of the government to have it made public. He was met by a counter request that he should not insist upon its omission from the printed votes, since the fact that his speech, which contained matters of complaint, was in print made the House deem it necessary to print the answer. The governor insisted upon his former message, and was informed that the House also insisted upon its position. He then told the House that the paragraph relating to the surveyor must be omitted, or he would use his prerogative as licenser of the press to prevent the printing of the " Remonstrance."[2] Again the House adhered to its former resolution, and thus the matter stood on the day of adjournment.[3] True to his threat, Governor Shute expressly commanded the printers of the province not to print the " Remonstrance." His order was a sufficient deterrent

---

[1] *General Court Records,* x. 417. On November 18, 1719, the "Additional Answer" of the representatives to the governor's speech was read in Council; whereupon the governor sent the secretary to the House with the message that he desired that "the said Additional Answer" should not be printed till he had considered it.

[2] The comments of Hutchinson (*Massachusetts,* ii. 209) are interesting: "He made a very great mistake. . . . This doctrine would have done well enough in the reigns of the Stuarts; in the present age, it is justly exceptionable; although by the liberty of the press we are not to understand a liberty of printing every thing, however criminal, with impunity."

[3] The proceedings in Council on December 10, 1719, when the governor and the House were exchanging messages as to the printing of the "Answer" by the House in its journal, are given in *General Court Records,* x. 450–451.

for Bartholomew Green, the former printer to the House;
but the representatives from Boston, who acted as a committee for the publication of the House Journal, induced
Nicholas Boone to print the votes with the objectionable
" Answer."[1]

Being thus defeated, the governor sought the advice of
his Council as to what he should do.   Sewall gives this
account of the Council's proceedings : —

> Jany 2 [1719–20].   Council: Govr asks Ad-
> vice what to say to Boon, who had printed the
> Deputies additional Answer to his Speech con-
> trary to his express Cõmand ?   Council made little
> answer, not knowing what to say.   Govr seem'd
> angry, and said he must Represent it home; he
> would leave no Stone unturn'd.   When the Govr
> gon, Mr. Belcher mention'd my reprimanding
> Mr. W[m] Dũmer, now Lt Govr, May, 1716; I said
> I did it by order of the Council.   Mr. Dudley
> mention'd his defence of Gov[r] Dudley ; I said
> twas answer'd.   Sir Edw. Northy said twas a Jest
> to think the Council ought to take on them the
> Governm[t]   I said twas harder to prove that Gov[r]
> Dudley did well to take the Government out of
> their Hands.[2]

Truly, this was half-hearted support for the governor's prerogative, and a significant change since the days when Paul
Dudley and William Dummer received summary treatment

---

[1] This " Answer " was not printed in the *News-Letter,* as stated in Palfrey,
New England, iv. 405; but that of March 20, 1720–21 (see below, p. 95),
was printed in both the *News-Letter* and the *Gazette.*   In the House Journal
as printed, the title-page contained these words: " Boston: Printed by N.
Boone, at the request and appointment of the Representatives of Boston, Mr.
Bartholomew Green, the former printer to the House, refusing to print the
same.   December 14, 1719 " (see article on " Liberty of the Press in Massa-
chusetts," *Boston Daily Advertiser,* May 12, 1882, p. 4).   It is noticeable that
Boone's bill for printing was paid without any visible trouble (see *General
Court Records,* xi. 132).

[2] *Sewall Papers,* iii. 238–239.

from the Council. The offending printer was not punished, and henceforth there could be no doubt that the House would print its proceedings as it pleased. The outcome meant that the exigencies of partisan warfare required defiance of the governor's pretensions. More than that, since the attorney-general and the Council appear to have declined to take any responsibility in the matter on the ground that there was no law to support a prosecution, it meant an official recognition that there was no legal censorship of the press in Massachusetts in 1720.[1] On this point, at least, royal instructions were not admitted to have the force of law *ex proprio vigore*.[2]

It will be remembered that the *News-Letter*, the first tolerated newspaper, came into being under official patronage, as an aid to Postmaster Campbell in his capacity of news-distributor. Indeed, the business opportunities of the postmaster's position made the publication of a news-

---

[1] Chalmers, *Revolt*, ii. 12, 19–20. No evidence has been found directly confirming the statement of Chalmers, which also appears in Palfrey, *New England*, iv. 405. A search in the Massachusetts archives and in the Record Office of London, and an examination of Add. Mss. 15486 in the British Museum (which consists of various papers relating to encroachments committed by the House of Representatives on the king's prerogatives, 1720–1724), have revealed nothing relating to censorship; nor does anything appear in the numbers of the *News-Letter* or the *Gazette* for that period. Nevertheless, the proposal of a licensing law, made by the governor a little later, is conclusive evidence that he had to admit the insufficiency of his instructions to give him the full power which he desired to maintain.

[2] It would appear that the opposite theory held good in New York, at least until after 1724 (see *New York Historical Manuscripts*, lxvi. 121). In Pennsylvania, Andrew Bradford seems not to have been subjected to restrictive censorship in general; but in 1721 he was haled before the Governor and Council for certain offensive publications, and was told that he "must not for the future presume to publish any thing relating to or concerning the Affairs of this Government, or the Government of any other of his Majestys Colonies, without the permission of the Governour or Secretary of this province, for the time being" (*Pennsylvania Records*, iii. 143, 145). In regard to the other colonies, no information on this point for this period has come to the author's knowledge.

paper one of his natural functions. However, when Mr. Campbell was displaced by a new appointee in 1719, he decided not to relinquish the *News-Letter*, "being still desired and encouraged to carry on the same by the Gentlemen, Merchants and others, his usual Customers." [1] His successor in office therefore started a second newspaper, the *Boston Gazette*, the first number of which appeared on December 21, 1719.[2] A permanent rivalry was now established in Boston journalism, since each succeeding postmaster took the management of the *Gazette* and Mr. Campbell continued the *News-Letter*. The new paper, like its older rival, had obtained the official sanction implied in the use of the phrase "published by authority." [3] Both of them, also, conformed to Massachusetts traditions by their genuine and respectable conservatism, and by their respectful deference to official authority. Even when they were drawn into service as opposing organs in political strife, and after they were emancipated from the scrutiny of licensers, their criticisms of officers and measures of government were most cautious.[4]

The years 1720 and 1721 were the period of an interesting development in one of the functions of newspapers. The journals as yet contained no editorials, no "letters to the editor," no reporters' comments upon current affairs, but included only a few commercial advertisements and brief colorless statements of what appeared to be accomplished facts of politics and "remarkable occurrences." Pamphlets had long been the only means of reaching the

---

[1] Thomas, *History of Printing*, ii. 17–18.

[2] Pennsylvania's first newspaper was published on December 22, 1719, the *American Weekly Mercury* being issued on that day.

[3] The circumstances of the appearance of the *Gazette* show that the new enterprise had no connection with the ending of censorship.

[4] Files of these papers have been examined in the libraries of the Massachusetts Historical Society and the American Antiquarian Society, and in the Lenox Library.

public with political arguments, and they were still the main reliance for that purpose. Now, however, the Boston papers began to print anonymous "advertisements," which were merely political articles expressing the views of those who paid for their insertion, and which were probably a less expensive and a more effective means than pamphlets were of advancing the agitation desired by their authors. Such transparent devices to avoid acknowledgment of personal responsibility were characteristic of a time when discussion was not really free but could not be wholly restrained.[1]

Throughout the ensuing year, the continued political conflicts were marked by more frequent and much freer use of the press.[2] Governor Shute, having been obliged to abandon the pretension that his instructions were a sufficient authorization to constitute him licenser of the press, was unable to control the obnoxious issues. He attempted, however, by the threat of criminal prosecutions, to make publishers cautious. Such was his policy in the case of John Colman, who published a small book in April, 1720, inquiring into the reasons for the depressed state of trade

[1] For example, the *Boston Gazette*, No. 30, July 11, 1720, contained an advertisement sarcastically criticising Elisha Cooke's recent pamphlet, *Just and Sensible Vindication*. The same issue printed an advertisement from the town of Tiverton that it had chosen as its representative in the next assembly a "gentleman of Known Ability and Reputation, and more especially famous for his Zeal in promoting Religion among us, and his very particular Respect to His Majesty's Government of New England." Nos. 62, 63, 65, and 67 of the same paper (February–March, 1720–21) contained advertisements of a distinctly political character by "Amicus Patriæ" and his opponents. London journalism was somewhat earlier in its development of what were known as "reflections" on current events. See Bourne, *English Newspapers*, i. chs. iii–iv.

[2] An account of the growth of the press in importance at this time is found in Winsor, *Narrative and Critical History*, v. 121, and in Bishop, *History of American Manufactures*, i. chs. vii–viii. See list of publications in Thomas, *History of Printing*, ii. 381–384.

in the province.[1] The governor laid the pamphlet before
the Council, which was " of opinion that the said pamphlet
contains in [it] many passages reflecting upon the Acts
and Laws of the Province and other proceedings of the
Government, and has a tendency to disturb the administration of the Government as well as the public peace."
Thereupon the board ordered Colman's arrest and prosecution ; and at the next term of the court of General Sessions
of the Peace he was accordingly proceeded against, as
shown in the records of that court for May 2, 1720 : —

> Upon an Informacōn from the Council Board
> to this Court at their Sessions on the Twenty
> fifth of April last past, that there had been
> Printed & published in Boston a Certain Pam-
> phlet Entituled the Distressed State of the Town
> of Boston &c Considered, In a Letter from a Gen-
> tleman in the Town to his Friend in the Country.
> Concerning which the Council Board (upon read-
> ing the same) were of Opinion, that the s.ᵈ Pam-
> phlet contains in it many Passages reflecting upon
> the Acts & Laws of the Province, & other pro-
> ceedings of the Governmᵗ and has a Tendency to
> Disturb the Administration of the Government, as
> well as the Publick Peace ; the Court then Ordered
> the s.ᵈ Pamphlet to be brought into the Court
> & Read, which was accordingly done   And John
> Colman of Boston Merchant being sent for, &
> Examined by the Court concerning the said
> Pamphlet, acknowledged that He the s.ᵈ Colman
> was the Authour thereof.   Whereupon it was
> then Considered by the Court, That the s.ᵈ John
> Colman should Recognize unto His Majesty in
> the sum of fifty pounds with two Sureties in the

[1] The sources for the case of John Colman are *Boston Gazette*, No. 17,
April 11, 1720; *News-Letter*, Nos. 834, 835, 836, April 11, 14, 18, 1720;
Council Records, vii. 132, April 12, 1720; *Records of General Sessions of the
Peace* (Mss.), 1719–1725, pp. 25, 29. For other controversial publications
brought out by the pamphlet, see advertisements in *Boston Gazette*, Nos. 21,
22, 23, 31; *News-Letter*, No. 836.

Sum of Twenty five pounds each   On Condition
that he should personally appear at the Court of
General Sessions of the Peace to be holden for
this County on the first Tuesday of July next, to
Answer to Such matters & things as should then
be objected against him on His Majesties behalf,
more especially relating to his being the Authour
& Publisher of the s.ᵈ Pamphlet & that he be of
the Good behaviour &c in yᵉ meantime.   But the
Declaring or Publishing of the s.ᵈ Order was continued until this time by Order of Court.   And
the s.ᵈ Order being now read & published in open
Court, He the s.ᵈ John Colman in the sum of
fifty pounds & Stephen Minot & James Gooch
both of Boston aforesaid Merch.ᵗˢ in the Sum of
Twenty five pounds each Recognized accordingly.[1]

For some unknown reason, the prosecution was not
pushed, but Colman was not released from his bonds
until July.[2]   In a similar manner, Benjamin Gray was
subjected to a prosecution the following year.[3]   His pamphlet, " A Letter to an Eminent Clergyman in the Massachusetts Bay," argued for bills of credit, declaring the
whole province "in a flame" because of the scarcity of
bills.   The Council voted that the book contained "many
vile, scandalous, and abusive expressions" which greatly
reflected on his Majesty's government, and that the author
should be prosecuted.   It further ordered that its vote
should be printed in the weekly papers.   Despite this
censure, Benjamin Gray advertised in the *Boston Gazette*
that "all Gentlemen, Tradesmen and others may be supplied by him with all the Pamphlets lately published."
This was taken as an act of defiance ; and, by order of the

[1] *Records of General Sessions of the Peace,* 1719–1725, p. 25.
[2] *Ibid.* 29.
[3] The sources for this case are *Boston Gazette,* Nos. 63, 65, February 27
and March 15, 1720–21; *Council Records,* vii. 236–237, 241–242; *Records of
Superior Court of Judicature,* 1719–1721, p. 356.

Council, Gray was bound over to answer for publishing the pamphlet, as well as for causing the advertisement to be printed in contempt of the former vote. The failure of the prosecution appears in the following entry of May 2, 1721: —

> Whereas Benjamin Gray of Boston in the County of Suffolk Bookseller was bound by Recognizance to appear at this Court to answer to such matters and things as should be objected against him on his Majesties behalf, more Especially for his Publishing a Pamphlet Entituled a Letter to an Eminent Clergyman in the Massachusetts Bay & for Causing an Advertise^mt to be printed in Contempt of a Note of the Council, as by the Recognizance on File. And the s^d Gray now appeared, & the Grand Jurors having found no Bill or present^mt against him; And he the s^d Gray having declared to the Court, that he had no design in Publishing & Printing the s^d Advertise^mt & Pamphlet, to Affront the Hono^ble Council; and likewise expressed his Sorrow for what he had done amiss; & humbly moving that he might be discharged from his s^d Recognizance, he was thereupon Discharged from the same by Proclamation.[1]

Governor Shute was evidently deeply concerned about the growing freedom of the press; for he sought to obtain from the General Court the establishment of censorship by a law of the province, explaining his views thus in his speech to the legislature on March 15, 1721: —

> I must observe to you that wee have been so unhappy of late as to have many Factious & Scandalous papers printed, & publickly sold at Boston, highly reflecting upon the Government, & tending to disquiet, the minds of his Majestie's Good Subjects, I therefore make no doubt but whoever is a Lover of the priviledges peace and

---

[1] *Records of Superior Court of Judicature,* 1719–1721, p. 356.

Good order of this province, will be very desirous to have a law made to prevent this pernicious and dangerous practice for the time to Come and more Especially since it is the King my masters positive Commands that no Book or paper, shall be printed without my Licence first obtained, which you have been lately acquainted with.[1]

Five days later the House replied to the governor in a very long " Answer," covering the many topics of his speech and having this to say about libels and licensing : —

It is an unhappy Circumstance attending a well Regulated Government, when they have Seditious and Scandalous Papers printed and publicly Sold or Dispersed.   And the most ready and effective way to prevent and hinder all such, is for the Executive part of the Government at the very first putting forth any such Factious Papers, strictly to endeavor the finding the Authors, thereof, that upon Conviction they may be brought to Condign Punishment, *That so others might hear and fear, and do no more so wickedly.* And Questionless when a certain Print, called *News from* Robinson Cruso's *Island,* was so publicly dispersed, and given to many Members of this House at the opening the session in *July* last, wherein the Contriver of the Piece not being content to compare the Representatives at their last May Sessions to a parcel of Men who in an angry humour did things on purpose to show their spite to your Excellency, and put a publjc affront upon you ; but goes on, and to compleat his Wickedness, gives the Lie to a Report of a Committee of both Houses, and a Resolve of this House sent to Mr. Agent Dummer, of the Twenty fourth of June, 1719, And these palpable Untruths he raises on the Transactions of that late Assembly, to induce the World to believe they had done things Ex Parte with a witness.   Had proper methods been then taken to discover and punish the Inventor

[1] *General Court Records,* xi. 113; *Boston Gazette,* No. 66, March 20, 1721.

or Publisher of that Libel; few or none afterward
would have dared to publish any others of that
Nature and Tendency.   Should an Act be made
to prevent the Printing any Book or paper, without Licence first obtained from the Governour for
the time being, no one can foresee the innumerable
inconveniencies and dangerous Circumstances this
People might Labour under in a little time.[1]

Notwithstanding the temper of the House, the Council
promptly passed an "Act for Preventing of Libels and
Scandalous Pamphlets, and for Punishing the Authors and
Publishers thereof."   The House, of course, negatived the
bill, for such action was part of its determined opposition
to the governor on many points. The governor soon found
it advisable to dissolve the unruly assembly, expressing,
among other complaints, his surprise that it should have
rejected the licensing bill, "the passing of which would . . .
have tended both to the Honour of the Government and
the Public Peace."   The next issue of the *News-Letter*
contained the full text of the "Answer of the House of
Representatives to His Excellency the Governor's Speech";
and his speech dissolving the General Court appeared at
the same time in the *Gazette*.[2]   Thus it was publicly announced to all that the press of Massachusetts was no
longer in subjection to any licensing authority.[3]

[1] The "Answer" from which the above extract is taken was adopted on
March 20.   The entire paper was printed in the *News-Letter*, No. 890, April
3, 1721.   Curiously enough, the records of the General Court for that date
contain no reference to the matter.

[2] Nothing about this speech appears in *General Court Records*, xi. 136,
which is the official account of the dissolution; but it was printed in the
Boston Gazette on April 3, and in the *News-Letter* on April 10, 1721.   See also
Hutchinson, *Massachusetts*, ii. 225.

[3] On Saturday, April 8, 1721, the Council took further action in regard to
rejected bills: —

"A Paper was read containing remarks upon two Bills pass'd in Council
at the last Session of the Gen. Assembly & non-concurred by the Representatives   The one entituled An Act for prevent⁵ Tumults & Riotous Assemblies

A third competitor in the Boston journalistic field made its appearance on August 17, 1721. From the first, this paper, the *New England Courant*, was more energetic and outspoken in its treatment of public affairs than its older rivals.[1] On account of the discomfiture of Governor Shute earlier in the year, James Franklin, its printer and publisher, was not obliged to seek the protection of the words " published by authority." Judged by the conservative standards of the time, whether from the social, the political, or the theological point of view, his newspaper existed chiefly as a vehicle of sedition. Increase Mather and Harvard College were the particular objects of ridicule by Franklin and his correspondents, especially at the time when Mr. Mather was exerting all his influence to introduce inoculation for the prevention of the small-pox plague that scourged Boston with painful frequency. The *Courant* violently opposed the movement by all the resources of argument and derision at the command of its clever contributors. Mr. Mather accosted the audacious printer in the street, and solemnly warned him that his wicked course

---

& for the more effectual Punishmᵗ of Persons guilty thereof, The other entituled An Act for the preventing Libels & Scandalous Pamphlets & punishing the Authours and Publishing thereof — Which said Remarks were accepted & approved of &

"Resolved That the same be forthwith published together with the aforesaid Bills" (*Council Records*, vii. 252). Unfortunately there is no trace of this publication, authorized by the Council, in the *News-Letter*, the *Gazette*, or the Archives.

Another short-lived General Court was dissolved by Governor Shute on July 20, 1721. His speech contained, among various other censures, another complaint against the House for its action in printing political papers. See *Massachusetts Acts and Resolves*, ii. 218; *Council Records*, xi. 207; Hutchinson, *Massachusetts*, ii. 235; *General Court Records*, xi. 198–199.

[1] Accounts of the *New England Courant*, of its establishment, its conduct, and its troubles, are found in Thomas, *History of Printing*, i. 110–112, ii. 31–38; Edward Everett, *Speeches*, ii. 43–46; Buckingham, *Reminiscences*, i. 49–88; Winsor, *Memorial History of Boston*, ii. 394–396; *Magazine of American History*, xvii. 4, 8–9.

H

in reviling ministers would bring upon him a judgment from God; but the warning merely served Franklin as a text for more stinging comments upon " one who is ever as groundless in his invectives as in his panegyrics." The irascible patriarch followed up his personal warning by a communication to the public, printed in the *Gazette*, advising the supporters of the *Courant* " to consider the Consequences of being Partakers in other Men's Sins, and no more Countenance such a Wicked Paper." He could " well remember when the Civil Government would have taken an effectual Course to suppress such a Cursed Libel, which, if it be not done, I am afraid that some Awful Judgment will come upon this Land, and the Wrath of God will arise, and there will be no remedy." Mather Byles, the grandson of Increase Mather, entered the lists to denounce the *Courant* as the production of the " Hell-Fire Club of Boston "; and Mr. Mather published a pamphlet to vindicate the ministry from the aspersions of these rasping critics, " these Profane Sons of Corah," these " Children of the Old Serpent." Franklin always retorted through the *Courant* with great effectiveness against " a reverend scribbler " who " quarrels with his neighbors because they do not look and think just as he would have them." The whole affair must have been a source of the keenest entertainment to provincial society, wholly unaccustomed as it had been to freedom of speech.

Perhaps Governor Shute was not ill-pleased to have some one besides himself suffer from the freedom of the press, which these obstinate people would not give him power to control; but such a free lance as the *Courant* could not long avoid incurring the wrath of the leading men if it did not eschew politics. The charge of connivance of the authorities in the operations of pirates was a tender point in Massachusetts in the first quarter of the eighteenth century. A sly insinuation in the *Courant* of

June 11, 1722, that the Massachusetts government was not earnestly coöperating for the capture of a pirate vessel then reported to be off the coast of New England, so exasperated the General Court that on the next day both houses denounced the item as a "high affront" to the government, and ordered the sheriff of the county of Suffolk to "forthwith Committ to the Goal in Boston the Body of James Franklyn Printer . . . there to remain during this Session."[1] A week's close confinement in the gloomy stone prison made Franklin ill, and induced him to present the following humble petition : —

> A Petition of James Franklyn Printer, Humbly Shewing that he is Truely Sensible & Heartily Sorry for the offence he has Given to this Court, in the late Courant, relating to the fitting out a Ship By the Government, & Truly Acknowledges his Inadvertency & Folly therein in affronting the Government, as also his Indiscretion & Indecency, when before the Court, for all which he Entreats the Courts forgiveness, & praying a discharge from the Stone Prison, where he is Confined, by Order of the Court, and that he may have the Liberty of the Yard, He being much Indisposed, & Suffering in his health, by the Said Confinement, — A Certificate from D: Zabdiel Boylstone of his Illness, being offered, with the Said petition.
> In the House of Representatives Read & Voted That James Franklyn now a Prisoner in the Stone Goal may have the Liberty of the Prison House & Yard, upon his Giving Security for his faithfull abiding there.
> In Council Read & Concurr'd — Consented to
> Sam:ll Shute [2]

Although the granting of his petition gave Franklin the liberty of the jail yard, he was not released from prison

---

[1] *General Court Records*, xi. 319–320; Appendix A below, p. 163.
[2] *Ibid.* 334 (June 20, 1722).

until the General Court was adjourned, three weeks later.[1] The Council had tried to take advantage of this opportunity to put the newspapers, at least, again under censorship. On July 5 it passed an order requiring "that no Such Weekly paper be hereafter printed or published, without the Same be first perused by the Secr^y. (as has been Usual)." Incorporated with this resolve was a vote that James Franklin should be put under bonds of one hundred pounds to be of good behavior until the end of the next session of the General Court. The members of the House were not to be tricked in this way, however; for they promptly refused to concur in the proposed order.[2]

The imprisonment of Franklin had no visible effect upon the freedom of comment allowed in the columns of the *Courant*. The week after his release the editor declared that he had never designed to affront the government, and promised that he would "proceed with the like caution" as long as he had the liberty of following his business. This editorial comment served, however, but as an introductory note for a stinging satire in doggerel verse on the action of the General Court in imprisoning him; the *Courant* for July 30 was largely devoted to a serious argument to prove from Magna Charta the illegality of the government's action; while a later issue contained an amusing parody on the Council resolution in which the House had refused to concur.

Apparently the partisan divisions caused by the opposition to Governor Shute had rendered it impossible to secure any action to restrain the "impudence" of Frank-

---

[1] This action by the General Court was an assertion of one form of legislative "privilege" — exemption from public criticism. Yet the term "privilege" does not seem to have been used in connection with the incident. The case is interesting, also, as an example of imprisonment on a legislative order, the confinement terminating with the end of the session.

[2] *General Court Records*, xi. 370; Appendix A below, p. 163.

lin; but early in 1723, after Governor Shute had sailed for England and left Lieutenant-Governor Dummer to wage the unprofitable war over the executive prerogative, the General Court again had its sensibilities strongly outraged by the *Courant.* The issue of January 14 contained no less than three "communications" of a nature to invite condemnation. The first of these was a mocking denunciation of religious hypocrites, intimating that New England contained not a small number of these detestable beings. The second deprecated the political contentions of the day, and spoke with especial regret of the departure of Governor Shute. The third assumed a position contrary to the second, spoke of the "extraordinary manner of Governor Shute's absenting himself from the government," suggested that he might be expected to labor in England against the interests of the province, and proposed that trusted agents be sent to England to vindicate the House of Representatives.

The two branches of the General Court were now able to act in unison, since the departure of the governor had removed the immediate cause of their differences. A joint committee of three from the Council and four from the House was appointed to consider and report what could properly be done to restrain the *Courant.* The committee censured the paper for its mockery of religion and its affront to the government, and recommended that the General Court should forbid James Franklin to "print, or publish the New England Courant, or any Pamphlet or paper of the like Nature, Except it be first Supervised, by the Secretary of this Province," and that bonds should be exacted from him for his good behavior. These recommendations were embodied in a joint order, which was passed to secure the desired end;[1] but Franklin neverthe-

---

[1] *General Court Records,* xi. 491, 493; Appendix A below, p. 164. For a "true copy" of the report of the committee, see *Suffolk Court Files,* No. 16461.

less brought out the *Courant* as usual, without having obtained a license, and even printed another satire on the government.[1] The Council promptly ordered his arrest for contempt of the General Court's order;[2] and to evade its requirements he had to resort to the subterfuge of causing the name of his brother, the young apprentice Benjamin Franklin, to be substituted, in the issue of February 11, for that of himself as publisher of the paper.[3] The ruse was successful, for the prohibitive order had been directed against James Franklin personally. The latter was next put under bonds to await the action of the grand jury for his publication of the *Courant* on January 21 without a license; but the attempt to indict him failed, and he was discharged from his bonds in May.[4] The paper then continued its vigorous existence, seemingly without further hindrance, until it died a natural death in 1727.[5]

The *Courant* case was of great importance in the development of freedom of the press, for it was the last instance of an attempt to revive and enforce censorship in Massachusetts. The prerogative of the governor as licenser had been set at defiance by the House, and his request to be given licensing powers under an act of the General Court had met with a negative response. Irritated by the *Courant,* the General Court had attempted to restrain its

---

[1] Sewall writes in his diary for January 21, "The Courant comes out very impudently" (*Sewall Papers*, iii. 319).

[2] *Council Records*, vii. 452-453 ; Appendix A below, p. 164. For the warrant issued for the arrest of Franklin, see *Suffolk Court Files*, No. 16480, and Appendix A below, p. 165. A deputy sheriff made return that he had searched diligently for the accused and could not find him, an indication that Franklin went into hiding for about two weeks to escape service of the writ.

[3] For a facsimile of that issue, see Winsor, *Memorial History of Boston*, ii. 395.

[4] *Records of General Sessions of the Peace*, 1719-1725, p. 186 ; *Records of Superior Court of Judicature*, 1721-1725, p. 119 ; Appendix A below, p. 165.

[5] No complete file of the *Courant* has been preserved.

freedom by requiring it to have a "customary" license from the secretary of the province; but, the press having outgrown its swaddling clothes, evasion of the order went unpunished, and restrictive censorship passed away.[1]

[1] Because of the importance of the *Courant* case as the last attempt to enforce censorship in Massachusetts, the original documents are given in full in Appendix A below. Together with the documents of the Checkley case (Appendix A below), they illustrate the forms and procedure of the eighteenth century, both in the General Court and in the lower courts of law.

CHAPTER VII.

LIMITED FREEDOM OF THE PRESS, 1723-1763.

THE prerogative of a provincial governor to control the press had rested upon the viceregal character of his office, — upon the king's prerogative as defined by long-standing custom and modified by the development of parliamentary control. Until invaded by the Long Parliament, the right of the crown to control the press without parliamentary enactments was unquestioned.[1] In the intervals during the reigns of Charles II and James II, when licensing acts were permitted to lapse, it was maintained that the common law and the prerogative were sufficient authorization for royal prohibition of printing without license;[2] but after the lapse of the last licensing act, in 1695, this right was no longer insisted upon in England, although the traditional function continued to receive recognition in the instructions of provincial governors.[3] What was more natural, then, than that the representative of the crown in a province should be unable to maintain his prerogative of control over the press as soon as it was seriously called in question?[4] Complaints to a home government that did not itself maintain this control would

---

[1] See chs. i-ii. above; also Paterson, *Liberty of the Press*, 44.

[2] See ch. iv. above; also Paterson, *Liberty of the Press*, 46, 55, and note.

[3] See ch. v. above.

[4] As Judge Mellen Chamberlain writes, in a letter to the author, "In the change of political, constitutional, and legal opinion, one would hardly look for consistency during the changes of administration, or in the same administration, for two consecutive years."

be met by a "most prudent silence," such as Chalmers says that the Board of Trade observed toward Shute's communications on this point.[1]

Not only from the legal point of view, but also from practical considerations of inability to enforce license regulations, it was manifest that a great change had been wrought in the status of the press. In the face of Governor Shute's experiences, the retention of the licensing clause in the instructions to his successor, Governor Burnet, was meaningless; and even the pretence of requiring censorship disappeared from the instructions of Governor Belcher, who entered upon the duties of his office on August 10, 1730.[2] In the province itself there was the frankest recognition of the new conditions, as two significant incidents prove. The first of these was the passage of an order by the Council, dated May 13, 1725, to the effect that "the Printers of the News Papers in Boston be ordered upon their Peril not to insert in their Prints any thing of the Publick Affairs of this Province relating to the War without the order of the Governm.ᵗ" [3]

[1] Chalmers, *Revolt*, ii. 20.

[2] Search in the papers of the Board of Trade, — in its *Journals*, xxxix–xli, and its *Miscellany*, v–vi, — has failed to reveal any statement of reasons for the omission of the licensing clause from the instructions of Governor Belcher; but, as the officials of the Board were often slow to recognize new developments in the functions of governors, the tardy omission of the licensing clause in instructions may be merely a characteristic example of routine neglect.

[3] *Council Records*, viii. 198. The following extract from the records of May 4, 1724 (*Ibid.* viii. 21), may be cited to show a similar state of affairs in that year : —

"Whereas an imperfect Acco.ᵗ relating to the Pirates was through a mistake inserted in the Boston Gazett published this day, which account ought not to have been in print;

"It is ordered that Mʳ Mulgrave, the Publisher of the s.ᵈ Gazette im̄ediately call in all the Papers that are gone out, that so yᵉ whole may be suppressed. W.ᵐ Dummer."

Compare the treatment of James Franklin for a like indiscretion about a pirate (above, p. 99).

This order, of course, plainly implies that other matters
could continue to be printed without such permission.
The regulation in itself, being a customary precaution to
prevent the publication of news of value to a belligerent
enemy, could hardly have been thought oppressive.   The
second incident grew out of a complaint by Dr. Timothy
Cutler, the Episcopalian clergyman, that the Boston *News-
Letter*, "published by authority," had misrepresented his
conduct of divine service.   Thereupon the Council took
action on September 2, 1725, as follows : —

> His Honour the Lieut! Governour laid before
> the Board a Memorial he received from D^r. Timo-
> thy Cutler complaining of an opprobrious Repre-
> sentation in the Boston News Letter (No. 1175
> published by authority) of his preaching and per-
> forming Divine Service according to ye usage of
> the Church of England at Scituate on the twenty
> eighth of July past,   That among ye many false-
> hoods & injurious reflections therein uttered there
> is this (However by the way this shews the Doc-
> tors fervent zeal & indefatigable pains to make
> Proselytes to ye Cause & promote Ceremonies by
> destroy^g substantials in Religion)   And desiring
> such reparation may be made to his Character, &
> protection afforded to the Church of England in
> this as well as all other Instances, as His Honour
> in his great wisdom & justice shall think fit —
>   Which Memorial being read & considered at
> the Board the following Vote passed Viz!
>   Whereas Inconveniences have once and again
> arisen to the Governmen! by several Matters be-
> ing printed in the News Letters that are said to
> be published by authority which were never known
> to the Governm! nor offered for their approbation.
>   Advised that His Honour the Lieut! Governour
> give his orders to the Publishers of the several
> Newspapers, not to insert in their papers these
> words (published by authority) or words of the
> like import for ye future.[1]

[1] *Council Records*, viii. 272–273.

Thus an admission by implication, in the one case, that the newspapers were not being supervised by censors was quickly followed by an explicit repudiation of official responsibility for issues of the press.[1] The meaning of the phrase "published by authority" had, however, changed so materially that the printers had come to regard its use as a valuable sanction of respectability and recommendation for reliability, and by 1729 had again made it necessary for the Council to enact this prohibition: —

> Ordered that the Printers of the News Papers be directed not to presume hence forward to insert in any part of their Prints that the same is published by Authority.[2]

Exemption from the intervention of a licenser before the act of printing was an important step in the development of freedom of the press; but it did not at once secure that measure of liberty which is the only true freedom of the press, — exemption from arbitrary prosecution, the benefit of just libel laws, and the acknowledged right of every person to use the press for reasonable discussion of all matters of public concern. If political prosecutions, such as those of John Colman and Benjamin Gray, resulted in defeat of the government, the fate of John Checkley proved that it was still exceedingly dangerous to publish religious opinions that were not in harmony with the pre-

---

[1] An examination of the files of the *News-Letter* shows that the words "published by authority" were dropped from the issue of July 18, 1720. This omission was probably a result of the dispute with Governor Shute, — of the use of the *News-Letter* by the opposition in fighting him, and of the defiance of his authority as licenser. On January 7, 1723, the words reappeared in the paper, doubtless because the enforcement of a licensing requirement was about to be attempted by the General Court, and the *News-Letter* sought protection. Finally, in 1725, in consequence of the orders of the Council, the words were again dropped.

[2] *Council Records*, ix. 189–190 (December 16, 1729).

dominant sentiment in the province.[1] In March, 1724, Checkley came to Boston with a stock of his printed book, " A Short and Easy Method with the Deists, with a Discourse concerning Episcopacy," which was doubtless substantially the treatise that he had been forbidden to print in Massachusetts five years before. The Council, declaring that the book contained "many vile and scandalous passages not only reflecting on the Ministers of the Gospel established in this Province, And denying their sacred Function & ye holy Ordinãces of Religion as administred by them, but also sundry vile insinuations against His Majestys rightfull and lawfull authority & the constitution of the Governm^t. of Great Britain," ordered the attorney-general to prosecute the author, and appointed special counsel to assist in the prosecution.[2] At the July session of the court of General Sessions of the Peace, Checkley was indicted, convicted, fined fifty pounds, and bound to good behavior.[3] He appealed to the Superior Court of Judicature, where a new trial followed and a second conviction resulted.

In its religious aspects, the Checkley case is a landmark in the history of Massachusetts, because, although the prosecution was successful, it was a hard-earned victory, and was the last instance in the commonwealth of legal persecution for defending Episcopacy. For the purpose of the present study the case is important, because even the brief and unsatisfactory records suggest certain features of the law of libel which became of great importance

---

[1] Checkley seems to have been regarded for some time as a contentious person. See above, ch. v.; also *Council Records,* vii. 116, 126, 135.

[2] *Ibid.* viii. 12–13 (March 19, 1723–24).

[3] *Records of General Sessions of the Peace,* 1719–1725, pp. 257, 268–273; *Suffolk Court Files,* No. 17865. For the long and verbose indictment, and additional documentary material, see Slafter, *John Checkley* (Prince Society, *Publications,* 1897). Certain of the more significant documents are reprinted in Appendix A below, pp. 166–171.

in English libel trials. The jury, for instance, did not bring in a general verdict of guilty, but found the following special verdict : —

> If the Book entituled a short and easy Method with the Deists Containing in it a discourse Concerning Episcopacy (Published & many of them sold by the s^d Checkley) be a false and Scandalous Libel — Then we find s^d Checkley Guilty of all and every part of the Indictm^t (Excepting that supposed to Traduce and draw into Dispute the undoubted right and Title of our sovereign Lord King George to the Kingdoms of Great Britain and Ireland and the Territorys thereto belonging) — But if the s^d Book Containing a discourse Concerning Episcopacy as afores^d be not a false & Scandalous Libel, Then we find him not Guilty.[1]

The libellous character of the publication being left to the court to decide as a matter of law, John Read, one of the ablest lawyers in the Province, counsel for the defendant, argued that his client ought to be acquitted on the special verdict. The first, second, and fourth divisions of his plea dealt with incidental technical matters. His third point was an endeavor to prove that the judges could not decide that the book was a libel, since the meaning and intent of the defendant ought to be cognizable by a jury only.[2] The unfortunate brevity of the reports leaves it uncertain whether or not Mr. Read was obliged to plead for the right of a jury in a libel trial to pass upon the whole issue, — that is, to bring in a general verdict decisive of both " law and fact." That right would have depended, of course, upon the nature of the instructions given by the court to the jury as to its functions, and these instructions are not preserved in the records ; but the argument that

---

[1] *Records of Superior Court of Judicature,* 1721–1725, p. 237.
[2] *Suffolk Court Files,* No. 18112 (1).

the court must recognize its own incompetence to pronounce a judgment of conviction under the terms of the special verdict certainly implied support of the doctrine that the jury must pass upon the criminality of the alleged libel.[1] Thus Mr. Read advocated a principle of the law of libel which the judges in Great Britain declined to recognize for more than sixty years, but which was at length vindicated by the eloquence of Erskine and established by Fox's declaratory act in 1792.[2] Mr. Read could hardly have expected to be sustained by the court, which decided, on the special verdict, that John Checkley was guilty, maintaining its own competence to resolve the question of libellous character as a matter of law involved in the special verdict.[3] If this decision did not follow a denial of the right of the jury to pass upon the whole issue, it constituted no danger to the freedom of the press, since the jury had the option, usual in other criminal cases, of rendering either a general or a special verdict. Massachusetts colonial legal practice shows no other cases which even suggest the grave danger to the independence of

[1] This important function of juries in libel cases was successfully maintained by William Bradford in his trial in Philadelphia in 1692. Against the contention of the prosecuting attorney, and despite the hostile attitude of his judges, Bradford got the court to charge the jury that it was to decide whether the publication in question tended to weaken the hands of the magistrates and to disturb the peace, as well as whether Bradford had actually printed the paper unlawfully. See Thomas, *History of Printing*, i. 211–222.

[2] Fox's Libel Act, 32 George III, c. 60. See May, *Constitutional History*, ii. 114–122. For a different interpretation of the issue created by Lord Mansfield's rulings, and of the effect of the Libel Act, see Forsyth, *History of Trial by Jury*, 223–235.

[3] John Checkley and his troubles are noticed in Winsor, *Narrative and Critical History*, v. 126, and in S. G. Drake's article on " Printers, Publishers, and Booksellers," in the *Historical Magazine*, April, 1870, p. 218. The fullest publication on the subject is Slafter's *John Checkley*, published by the Prince Society in 1897. The Boston Public Library has a pamphlet (*3544.22), published in London in 1730, giving Checkley's speech at the trial, the jury's verdict, the plea in arrest of judgment, and the sentence of the court.

juries and to the freedom of the press involved in Lord Mansfield's famous rulings in English libel cases.

By 1723 the press of Massachusetts had attained only so much of freedom as enabled it, in its further development, to keep pace with the intellectual, religious, and political independence of the commonwealth.[1] The interval between the difficulty with the *New England Courant* and the dissatisfaction with Governor Shirley's administration was singularly free from any contests over freedom of discussion in the press. The reasons for this cessation of strife were twofold. In the first place, there was general acquiescence in the toleration of cautious pamphlets and of the colorless newspapers of the day. In the second place, since the discontinuance of the *Courant* and the departure of James Franklin for Rhode Island, no printer in Massachusetts had had the spirit to publish anything like fearless criticism of public measures. The sharp political disputes of the day, such as those over the governor's salary and the issue of bills of credit, were presented in the newspapers almost wholly by the official speeches, addresses, and writings of both sides.[2] The press can hardly be said to have been directed by editors, — in the present meaning of that term, — when publishers were accustomed to recommend their journals to the public on the ground that both sides of every question would be allowed an equal hearing, without any attempt to present

[1] An illuminating account of general political and literary conditions in New England to the beginning of the eighteenth century is given by Barrett Wendell in his *Literary History of America*, bk. i. His concluding sentence (p. 55) is this, " In history and in literature alike, the story of seventeenth-century America is a story of unique national inexperience." See also Tyler, *History of American Literature*.

[2] The numbers of the *New England Weekly Journal* in the library of Harvard University show that between 1727 and 1731, only one original letter (in the issue of July 7, 1729) was published to present the assembly's side of the dispute over the governor's salary. It is a very mild argument.

editorial opinions. The proprietors of newspapers were, for the most part, content to regard themselves as mere printers, business agents, or managers of papers virtually edited by joint action of their customers. As one of them said, "I am of no Party, but act purely as a Printer, and would as soon serve one Side as the other."[1] It required a long apprenticeship for the directors of newspapers to become editors, able and willing to formulate and even to educate public opinion.[2]

Thomas Fleet, printer and publisher of the *Evening-Post* from 1735 to 1758, was the most enterprising journalist in Boston during his long career. It was not his purpose to engage in controversies; but he was willing to print vigorous articles from writers of different views, and he was not above using the commonest personal abuse toward those who criticised him. He showed some little editorial capacity in the selection of miscellaneous articles to reprint from contemporaneous newspapers, and he occasionally indulged in brief, sarcastic comments on current items of news. He recognized the significance of

[1] Thomas Fleet, in the *Evening-Post*, March 30, 1741.

[2] The provincial character and halting development of journalism in the American colonies before the Revolution, as contrasted with the progress and influence of English journalism in the eighteenth century, may be seen by comparing Hudson, *Journalism*, chs. i–vi., Buckingham, *Reminiscences*, i., and Thomas, *History of Printing*, with Bourne, *English Newspapers*, i. chs. iii–vi. There was no rivalry in journalism in Pennsylvania until 1728, and none in New York until 1733. Newspapers were established in Maryland in 1727, South Carolina in 1732, Rhode Island in 1733, Virginia in 1736; but some of these ceased publication after brief intervals of struggle against inadequate support. Public interest in the last great war for national control in America stimulated the establishment and support of newspapers. Between 1755 and 1764 there were various new journals in New Hampshire, Rhode Island, Connecticut, Virginia, North Carolina, South Carolina, and Georgia, besides a few more started in Massachusetts, New York, and Pennsylvania. The pre-Revolutionary controversies with the mother country had a similar effect in developing colonial journalism.

the trial of Peter Zenger for libel in New York,[1] by printing an account of it, in justification of "The Liberty of
the Press," in the *Evening-Post* for May 29, 1738. Quoting from the pamphlet in which Zenger described his
experiences, the article closes with Mr. Hamilton's plea
to the jury to secure "the Liberty, both of exposing and
opposing *arbitrary Power*, (in these Parts of the World, at
least) by *speaking* and *writing* TRUTH." The use of the
columns of the *Post* for the publication of all sorts of
opinions, orthodox or heterodox, serious or sarcastic,
evoked a great deal of criticism from the conservative
element in Boston. Preachers took occasion to denounce
Fleet as a mercenary corrupter of good morals, and to
advise the magistrates to suppress his paper as "a dangerous engine, a sink of sedition, error, and heresy." One
minister warned his people against reading such news-

---

[1] This famous case occurred in 1734–1735. It was an outcome of the bitter
partisan quarrels of Governor Cosby's administration, Zenger being merely the
agent of the powerful leaders of the opposition. William Bradford's *New
York Gazette*, published since 1725, had been uniformly an administration
organ. Zenger's *Weekly Journal* was started in November, 1733, to give the
opposition party a regular vehicle of communication with the public. Its
contributors and supporters justified their frank and caustic discussion of current politics in dissertations upon the freedom of the press. Being unable to
punish the real authors of the "libels," Cosby and the Council prosecuted
Zenger for his temerity in publishing them. The trial was noteworthy because
of the maintenance by the court of the sound common-law doctrine that the
defendant could not plead the truth of the alleged libel as a justification. The
skill of Zenger's lawyer, Mr. Andrew Hamilton, secured his acquittal by adroit
appeals to the sympathies of the jury; and the result was heralded as a vindication "of the rights of mankind and the liberty of the press." In the development of public opinion toward that end, the case was indeed a contributing
influence, but it did not secure freedom of the press even in New York, and,
despite Fleet's quotation of Zenger's narrative, it had no apparent effect upon
the law and practice of Massachusetts. There are many accounts of the
affair in the standard histories of New York, in Thomas, *History of Printing*,
etc. See also *New York Colonial Documents*, vi. *passim ;* files of the *Weekly
Journal* in the library of the New York Historical Society ; contemporaneous pamphlets in the New York State Library.

I

papers and pamphlets as contained religious controversies. The *Post's* answers to these gentlemen attested Fleet's powers of recrimination. He rejoiced that the people were no longer enveloped in ignorance, and said: "The next stroke may probably be at the *Liberty of the Press.* And what a fine introductiᵥ ᵧ 's will be to *Popery*, we leave our readers to judge."[1]

This kind of freedom of discussion about matters that did not have an official connection with the government's policy was too well recognized to be a cause for prosecution; but it was still easy for printers to publish comments on political matters that were liable to lead to trouble. Thomas Fleet found himself the object of such attention in March, 1742, when the *Evening-Post* contained a news item giving a reported conversation with a naval officer, to the effect that Parliament had called for all the papers relating to the war, and that "twas expected that the Right Honble Sir Robert Walpole would be taken into custody in a very few days." The next day Fleet was examined by the Council, which resolved that the paragraph was a scandalous and libellous reflection upon his Majesty's ad-

---

[1] Buckingham, *Reminiscences*, i. 134. Political controversies with Governor Clinton and Lieutenant-Governor Colden, in 1746–1747, drew from the assembly of New York interesting expressions favorable to liberty of the press. Governor Clinton, for instance, forbade Parker to reprint in the *Gazette* a certain remonstrance of the assembly. Thereupon the House passed this resolution, with several others : "*Resolved*, Nemine Contradicente, That his Excellency's Order to forbid the printing or re-printing the said Remonstrance, is unwarrantable, arbitrary and illegal, and not only an open and manifest Violation of the Privileges of this House, but also of the Liberty of the Press, and evidently tends to the utter Subversion of all the Rights and Liberties of this House, and of the People they represent" (*New York Assembly Journal*, 1743-1765, pp. 193, 198). In 1755 the Pennsylvania assembly also asserted its independence of the executive in the matter of ordering papers to be printed (*Pennsylvania Records*, vi. 322–328). These controversies, like those between Governor Shute and the Massachusetts House of Representatives, were essentially contests for legislative privilege against executive domination, not for freedom of the press.

ministration, and, therefore, ordered the attorney-general to file an information against Fleet and to prosecute him.[1] For some unknown reason, the prosecution was not pushed;[2] but the action showed the purpose of the Council to restrain political news-writers within narrow bounds.

In October, 1754, the House of Representatives had occasion to assert the privilege of its members to be free from annoying public criticism.[3] Some one had published an anonymous pamphlet entitled "The Monster of Monsters," containing a satirical account of the debates of the House upon an unpopular excise bill. The pamphlet was really nothing more than a harmless piece of humor; but the House did not so regard it. After hearing it read, the affronted representatives resolved that it was a false, scandalous libel, reflecting upon the proceedings of the House in general and on the members in particular. The hangman was ordered to burn it in King Street below the courthouse, and the messenger was required to see the order carried out. Daniel Fowle, being suspected as printer of the libel, was brought before the House and with his apprentice was subjected to examination. He was not dis-

---

[1] *Council Records*, x. 583–584 (March 9, 1741–42).

[2] Thomas (*History of Printing*, ii. 48) says that Fleet produced witnesses to prove the truth of the paragraph, and therefore escaped prosecution.

[3] The following proclamation shows that in April, 1751, the General Court had been scandalized by public criticism : —

"Whereas there has been lately published & dispersed within this Province an Anonymous printed Paper in the Form of a Ballad, called A Sad & deplorable Lamentation wherein are contained many Expressions horribly prophane & impious, and such also as reflect the greatest Indignity & Contempt upon the Authority of this Legislature, & which tend very much to weaken if not subvert the happy Constitution of this Governm.t And whereas one Robert Howland of Duxbury & one Fobes Little of Little Compton are informed against for industriously publishing & dispersing & one or both of them be strongly suspected to be the author of the Paper aforesaid

"I do therefore [order their arrest, and proclaim a reward of ten pounds for the capture of either.

"S. Phips]." — *Massachusetts Archives*, lviii. 365–366, cii. 598.

posed to show any contempt of authority, and was easily led into confessions which convinced his accusers that he had been concerned in publishing the pamphlet; whereupon, by order of the House, the speaker issued his warrant for the imprisonment of Fowle in the common jail. The statement of Daniel Fowle having implicated his brother Zechariah, as well as Mr. Royal Tyler, the speaker had them also taken into custody. Mr. Tyler demanded to be allowed counsel, and when this was denied him he declined to answer the questions put to him. His additional request to be released on bail was likewise refused, and he spent two days in jail while the House considered his case. Zechariah Fowle escaped imprisonment through illness; but his brother Daniel remained for two days closely imprisoned, and three days more in custody in the jailer's house. He was then brought before the House, reprimanded by the speaker, and sent back to confinement until he should pay the costs of the case. The next day he was allowed to go to see his anxious wife, on his promise to be at hand whenever he should be summoned. He was not sent for, and the prosecution was dropped.[1]

---

[1] The assemblies of New York and Pennsylvania also endeavored to maintain their privilege to be free from public criticism. Hugh Gaine, having without authorization printed a part of the proceedings of the New York assembly in his newspaper, the *Me ury*, on November 12, 1753, was summoned to the bar, humbly sued for pardon, and was dismissed with a reprimand from the speaker (*New York Assembly Journal*, 1743–1765, pp. 358–359). The Reverend Hezekiah Watkins, author of an article in the *New York Gazette or Weekly Post-Boy* of March 15, 1765, was arrested by the sergeant-at-arms and reprimanded (*Documentary History of New York*, iv. 209). Alexander McDougall was punished, in 1770–1771, as the reputed author of a printed paper which censured the New York assembly for one of its votes (*New York Assembly Journal*, 1766–1776, pp. 39–42; *New York Colonial Documents*, viii. 213; *Documentary History of New York*, iii. 323). The Reverend Dr. Smith, provost of the Academy of Philadelphia, was imprisoned in 1757, upon the order of the assembly of Pennsylvania, for publishing a libel relating to its proceedings (*Pennsylvania Records*, viii. 438 ff.). Compare these incidents with the earlier contests of assemblies for legislative privilege to publish their own proceedings.

Fowle was not willing to submit quietly to this arbitrary treatment, however, and turned the occasion to some profitable account by publishing a pamphlet entitled " A Total Eclipse of Liberty," in which he narrated his troubles with all the pathos he could command, asserting that his prosecutors had kept him confined for six days " in that cold, lonesome, dark, and horrible prison without any fire, not suffering any person to assist him or to speak to him." In May, 1755, he instituted a suit in the Inferior Court of Common Pleas for one thousand pounds damages by illegal imprisonment, naming as defendants Thomas Hubbard, the speaker who had issued the warrant of imprisonment, William Baker, the messenger who had arrested him, and Alexander Young, the under-keeper of the jail. Jeremiah Gridley, attorney for the defence, put in a plea that in the arrest and imprisonment of Fowle by order of the House, his clients had acted lawfully in their several capacities, and that therefore the action must be dismissed with costs against the plaintiff. Richard Dana, attorney for Fowle, maintained that the official positions of the defendants did not bar an action against them for unlawful acts, even although it was alleged that they proceeded in course of their duties, for the injured party must be accorded his right to have his cause judicially determined by the courts. Mr. Gridley put in a rejoinder reënforcing the points he had made, and then the court took the point of law under advisement. In the January session, 1756, a decision was rendered barring the action and assessing the costs against Fowle. An appeal was immediately taken to the Superior Court of Judicature, where the case was continued through three successive sessions, or until February, 1757, when the final judgment was rendered, sustaining the plea in bar, and assessing still larger costs against the unfortunate printer.

More than a year before the case reached its final determination, Daniel Fowle had emigrated from Massachusetts to Portsmouth, New Hampshire, to become the first printer in that province.   The writ of execution against him for eight pounds, nineteen shillings, and sixpence was returned by Sheriff Greenleaf in August, 1757, with the endorsement that he could find neither property nor the body of Fowle in his precinct.   For five years the collection of the bill of costs was not pushed; but then Fowle was sued for the amount in New Hampshire.   Thereupon he petitioned the General Court of Massachusetts that the judgment of costs against him might be declared void, and that a money allowance for his suffering might be given him.   His petition recited the occasion and the method of his arrest and imprisonment, and expressed the belief that most of the persons concerned in the affair had "long since been convinced he was innocent."   No attention having been paid to this petition, Fowle again, in 1764, appealed to the General Court for relief; whereupon it was voted that the costs should be remitted to him, and that the accounts of the gentlemen who had acted for the House should be paid out of the public treasury.   By authority of this vote, a warrant for thirty-one pounds, seven shillings, was issued to Fowle on August 21, 1765, "to discharge his account for sundry expenses occasioned by his being taken up and imprisoned on suspicion of printing a pamphlet called 'The Monster of Monsters.'"   But this did not satisfy Fowle, who again, in 1766, petitioned for some further recompense. The remittance of costs had been but a partial relief, he said, since he had never had a trial of the merits of his cause, but had been "debarred from his action on the supposition that the House had the inherent right to commit him . . . by their general warrant."   He thought that the aggravated circumstances attending his commitment should entitle him to favorable consideration, since "the most august Court of the British Nation, when a Cause of a similar Nature was the object of their Attention, and after a learned and full Debate, wisely determined in Favour of the Complainants." [1]   This appeal touched a responsive chord at a time when the feelings of the people had been much excited by the enforcement of trade laws and by the Stamp Act; and Fowle obtained twenty pounds "on account of his sufferings." The House was ready to give relief to one who could recommend himself to sympathy in the name of liberty; while the Governor and Council found no cause for opposing a vote which tended to reflect upon the wisdom of a former House.[2]

Previous to 1755 the press of Massachusetts had not been hampered by stamp or advertisement taxes; but in January of that year a province act was passed levying duties upon vellum, parchment, and paper, one paragraph taxing every printed news-sheet one halfpenny.[3]   Such

[1] See resolutions of the Commons, April 22, 1766, in Cobbett, *Parliamentary History*, xvi. 209. These resolutions grew out of the cases of Wilkes and the printers involved in the prosecutions connected with the *North Briton*, No. 45 (see May, *Constitutional History*, ch. xi).

[2] The proceedings against Daniel Fowle, Joseph Russell, Zechariah Fowle, and Royal Tyler are in the *House Journal*, under dates October 24, 25, 26, 1754. The records of the General Court do not contain this material, probably because it relates to House proceedings only. Additional manuscript sources are: *Suffolk Court Files*, Nos. 74517, 74879, 75205, 75334, 77371; *Records of Superior Court of Judicature*, 1757–1759, p. 24; *Massachusetts Archives*, lviii. 476, 502, 556; *General Court Records*, xxv. 268–269, xxvi. 340; *Council Records*, xvi. 35, 176–177. The subject is treated in Thomas, *History of Printing*, i. 129–134; Minot, *Massachusetts*, i. 206–213; Buckingham, *Reminiscences*, i. 159–162; Drake, *Boston*, 635; Winsor, *Memorial History of Boston*, ii. 404 note, and *Narrative and Critical History*, v. 177; Barry, *Massachusetts*, ii. 249–250. The Boston Public Library has the *Monster of Monsters*, the *Total Eclipse of Liberty*, and the *Appendix to A Total Eclipse of Liberty*. The third and last petition of Fowle is reproduced in Appendix A, below, pp. 171–173.

[3] *Massachusetts Acts and Resolves*, iii. 794, 834; *House Journal*, 1755–1756, pp. 32, 42. The act is printed, and the stamps are described, in *New England Historical and Genealogical Register*, xiv. 267; for a note on this stamp act, see Winsor, *Narrative and Critical History*, v. 177. New York had a

taxes had been imposed by the government in England ever since 1712, with the avowed intention of limiting the circulation of cheap papers and preventing the issue of libels by irresponsible printers.[1] Although there is no evidence that the provincial measure was meant to serve any similar political purpose, the law nevertheless bore hard upon the newspapers, whose subscription rates had to be increased; while one paper, the *Boston Gazette or Weekly Advertiser,* was discontinued on account of the tax.[2] Another journal, the *Boston Gazette or Country Journal,* was led to argue for the freedom of the press by printing articles on that subject extracted from its London contemporaries. In one such article, the principle was broadly maintained that freedom to communicate one's sentiments to the public "in that manner which may make them most universally known," is essential to the liberty of the subject and "coeval with all free governments"; and in another the assertion was made that the original and true cause which led Parliament to overthrow Charles I was his "suppression of the liberty of the press." "Had not Prynn lost his Ears," says this writer, "King Charles would have never lost his Head."[3] Such agitation as this caused the abandonment of so unpopular a tax, which expired by limitation, and ceased to be levied on May 1, 1757.[4]

similar tax from 1756 to 1760: see *New York Assembly Journal,* 1743–1765, p. 522; *Laws of New York,* 1691–1773, p. 370.

[1] Bourne, *English Newspapers,* i. 81; May, *Constitutional History,* ii. 108, 172, 214, 215; Collet, *History of the Taxes on Knowledge.*

[2] *New Jersey Archives,* xii. p. cxlvii. During the levy of this tax there were three newspapers in Boston, all of which used the stamps.

[3] Issues of May 26 and June 2, 1755.

[4] Fleet's *Evening-Post,* No. 1127, April 4, 1757, bearing the required stamp, contained this notice : —

"Gentlemen,   "To the Customers for this Paper.

"As the Stamp-Act will expire the second Day of May next, (after which there will be some Abatement of the present Price, notwithstanding the very

The liberal ideas upon the proper freedom of the press evoked by reaction against the provincial stamp act were not endorsed by Governor Shirley or his associates in the executive branch of the government.[1] On the contrary, they were very much disturbed when popular dissatisfaction with the administration of the French and Indian War found expression in the newspapers, and when New York and Boston journalists engaged in wordy recriminations over the late expedition against Crown Point.[2] In 1756 the governor sent to both houses a special message upon the "licentiousness" of the press, recommending that measures be taken to prevent the publication of "malignant libels" tending to alienate the affections of the several provinces from each other. The General Court answered the message by expressing disapprobation of the writings in question, and professing a willingness to countenance a prosecution of the offenders. It said that it

high Price of Paper, &c. since the War) the Publisher thinks it proper to inform you that he will send out no Papers to any one who does not clear off all Accounts to that Time."

[1] The subservience of newspaper editors to the prejudices of their patrons is shown by the proceedings of the selectmen of Boston, on March 16, 1757. After giving Edes and Gill, of the *Gazette*, an order to print the votes of the town, they said to Mr. Edes : "You have printed Such Pamphlets & such things in your News Papers as reflect grossly upon the receivd religious principles of this People which is verry Offensive and Complaints have been made to us by some of the Inhabitants concerning S^d. Phamplets & papers we therefore now Inform you if you go on printing things of this Nature you must Expect no more favours from Us. To which Mr. Edes answerd to the following Effect. That He was sorry He had given Occasion to any Persons to be Offended at what He had printed, but that he would take more care for the future, & publish nothing that shall give any uneasiness to any Persons whatever." See Boston Record Commissioners, *Nineteenth Report, 1754–1763*, pp. 54–55.

[2] The printers of newspapers in Boston had been prohibited, on September 6, 1755, from publishing anything on the expedition against Crown Point without permission of the General Court, or in the recess of the Court, of the Governor and Council. See *Massachusetts Acts and Resolves*, iii. 947.

would even consent to supply any defect in the laws on the subject, and hoped that the government of New York would " restrain the licentiousness of the press" in that province.[1] No action resulted from this interchange of communications; and newspaper warfare continued to develop naturally, with a growing boldness corresponding to the intensity with which political issues were contested.

[1] Minot, *Massachusetts*, i. 268–270, quoting from *House Journal*. Complaints of newspaper publications about the war were likewise made in New York and Pennsylvania in 1757. Sir Charles Hardie wrote in 1756, "And tho' I am aware how clamerous the World is in being denied the Liberty of the Press, that shall not discourage me, as I am certain such a Licentiousness is Incompatible with the Publick Service" (*Pennsylvania Records*, vii. 339); and in 1757, Lieutenant-Governor Denny suggested, "Perhaps it may even be thought necessary for His Majesty's Service, that Articles of Intelligence should receive my Approbation, and not [be] published without Leave" (*Ibid.* 447).

CHAPTER VIII.

REVOLUTIONARY FREEDOM AND CONSTITUTIONAL GUARANTEES, 1763-1789.

THE political agitation consequent upon the new colonial policy of the British ministry after 1763 gave an added importance to the press as a means of influencing public opinion;[1] and the degree of freedom enjoyed by the press of Massachusetts in particular allowed a very effective use of local newspapers by the "patriot" leaders in their "campaigns of education."[2] The *Boston Gazette*, published by Edes and Gill, became the recognized organ for the presentation of grievances on all occasions. James Otis, Samuel Adams, John Hancock, Joseph Warren, Thomas Cushing, John Adams, and Josiah Quincy, Jr., concealing their identity under fictitious names, were some of its contributors and ardent supporters. With a freedom of criticism which could not be restrained, they formed public sentiment and led the opposition to all arbitrary measures. Yet, with all their boldness, they knew that they were always in danger of prosecution; and the offi-

[1] On the issues of the colonial press to 1775, see lists of "Ante-Revolutionary Publications" in Thomas, *History of Printing*, ii. The same volume gives many particulars of the rise of colonial newspapers, which are supplemented by William Nelson's "Account of Early American Newspapers," published in the *New Jersey Archives*, xi, xii, xix. See also Evans, *American Bibliography*, ii. The best analysis of the literature of the Revolutionary era is that by Tyler, *Literary History of the American Revolution*.

[2] The press in the rest of the thirteen colonies was used in a similar manner by the several constituencies. See Tyler, *Literary History of the American Revolution*, i. *passim*.

cers of the crown, too, thought that successful prosecution of the malignant authors and publishers was a distinct possibility. John Adams accorded to Edes and Gill great praise for printing articles on public questions, since "the arm of power," said he, "is always stretched out, if possible, to destroy the freedom of thinking, speaking, and writing;" and he urged them not to be intimidated from publishing with the utmost freedom anything warranted by the laws of the country.[1] As the imperial Stamp Act of 1765 would have been a heavy burden upon newspapers if it had been enforced,[2] the printers had a special reason for encouraging universal resistance to the execution of the law. Their interest in the matter received unusual notice from at least one source in Massachusetts, when the town of Worcester instructed its representatives in the General Court, in June, 1765, to "take special care of the LIBERTY OF THE PRESS."[3] Instead of paying the stamp tax, the newspapers became only the more ready to join in the opposition to the government's unpopular measure.[4] Until relief came with the repeal of the act, the Boston publishers were bold enough to issue their papers without stamps and without resort to technical evasion of the law.

The current of adverse criticism which was directed against Chief Justice Hutchinson in 1767 made him resolve that he must check the growing licentiousness of the press, by publicly defining the legal limits of its freedom. His charge to the grand jury at the August term of the Supe-

---

[1] John Adams, *Works*, iii. 457.

[2] Drake, *Boston*, 708 note.

[3] *Boston News-Letter*, June 4, 1765 ; Buckingham, *Reminiscences*, i. 31.

[4] The non-enforcement of the Stamp Act made possible the irregular appearance of newspapers and handbills in several of the colonies, without the use of the required stamps. The proprietors of some journals suspended publication, while others evaded the law by issuing news-sheets headed "Remarkable Occurrences," or without titles. See Thomas, *History of Printing*, ii. 10, and *passim ;* also *New Jersey Archives*, xi. p. cix.

rior Court of Judicature contained the following significant passages : —

> Pretty high Notions of the Liberty of the Press, I am sensible, have prevailed of late among us; but it is very dangerous to meddle with, and strike at this Court.
>
> The Liberty of the Press is doubtless a very great Blessing; but this Liberty means no more than a Freedom for every Thing to pass from the Press without a Licence. — That is, you shall not be obliged to obtain a Licence from any Authority before the Emission of Things from the Press. Unlicenced Printing was never thought to mean a Liberty of reviling and calumniating all Ranks and Degrees of Men with Impunity, all Authority with Ignomimy. — To carry this absurd Notion of the Liberty of the Press to the Length some would have it — to print every Thing that is Libellous and Slanderous — is truly astonishing, and of the most dangerous Tendency.[1]

Then the chief justice went on to say that he did not mention the matter in order to ask the grand jury to present indictments at this time, but that he merely wished to caution people that they would be summarily punished for contempt if they should show disrespect to an " executive court." The special occasion of these threats was the publication in the *Evening-Post* of July 6 and 13, 1767, of certain articles by Joseph Hawley commenting upon a recent decision of the court. Mr. Hawley was not at once proceeded against for contempt; but at the September term, in Springfield, he was dealt with sternly by the chief justice, as shown by the following record : —

> Two peices subscribed, Joseph Hawley, containing divers injurious and scandalous Reflections on several of the Justices of this court, for what they

---

[1] Quincy, *Massachusetts Reports*, 244. Yet the opposition charged that the chief-justice wished to see censorship introduced again.

did in Court, and as Justices thereof, having been printed and published in the Boston Evening post, of the 6th and 13th, of July last, and it appearing to the Court, upon the examination of Joseph Hawley Esqr in open Court, that he was the Author of those peices: Its therefore Ordered by the Court that his name be struck out of the Rolls of the Barristers and Attorneys of the Court, & that he do not hereafter appear or act as a Barrister or Attorney of this Court.[1]

The events of the next few months did not tend to diminish the vigor of political agitation. Governor Bernard was denounced in the *Boston Gazette* as the enemy of the province, while Hutchinson was made the object of direct attack. The latter's claim to be a member of the Council *ex officio*, since he held the office of lieutenant-governor, was complained of by the House as "a new and additional instance of ambition and a lust of power." On December 10, 1767, Israel Mauduit wrote to him from London in the following words : —

Before the Arrival of this you will know, that orders are gone from Lord Shelbourns office to prosecute the Printers of that treasonable Letter to Edes and Gill in your Gazette of the 31st August last. What Mr Barnard will do in it I cant say, or what your Juries may think of it; But if they should find a Bill against such Incendiary papers, Sure I am that the town of Boston cant do a better thing, more Effectually to Erace the ill Impression made by their former Riotings, and to reinstate themselves in the good opinion of the Publick : If indeed your people desire it; for in some of the papers from your Representatives they seem to pretend a concern for our good Opinion meerly to express their Contempt of it.[2]

[1] *Records of Superior Court of Judicature*, 1767–1768, p. 46.
[2] *Massachuset's Archives*, xxv. 237–238.

Under the circumstances, the futility of the threatening orders from Lord Shelburne's office was soon made apparent. Because the governor secured a letter from Secretary of State Shelburne censuring the opposition in the House, he was pilloried with violent vituperation by an anonymous contributor in the *Gazette* of February 29, 1768. The communication was couched in such extreme language that the Council at once answered the governor's message submitting the libel to its consideration, by declaring that it could not but look upon the article with the utmost abhorrence and detestation;[1] to which the governor replied that he should not have heeded the attacks of an anonymous libeller, if he had not felt that it was " pregnant with Danger to the Government." He then laid the matter before the House, which expressed regret that any publication in a newspaper should give the governor any apprehension of danger to the government, but declared that, as the letter in question did not name any particular person, it did not feel justified in taking any further notice of the matter, especially since ample provision for the punishment of offenders already existed in the laws. As one branch of the legislative, it was ready, it said, to discountenance the abuse of freedom; but it asserted, as no Massachusetts legislative body ever before had done, that " the Liberty of the Press is a great Bulwark of the Liberty of the People: It is therefore the incumbent Duty of those who are constituted the Guardians of the People's Rights to defend and maintain it." [2]

The governor continued to remonstrate, but the opposition rejoiced in an untrammelled press. The *Gazette* of March 14, 1768, printed two communications praising the stand taken by the House. One letter read: " With Pleasure I hear the general Voice of this People in favor

---

[1] *Council Records*, xvi. 293 (March 1, 1768).

[2] Quincy, *Massachusetts Reports*, 270–276; Bradford, *State Papers*, 113–121.

of freedom; and it gives me solid satisfaction to find all
orders of unplaced independent men, firmly determined,
as far as in them lies, to support their own RIGHTS, and
the Liberty of the PRESS." The second article commended
the *Gazette* for printing articles against the Stamp Act
and other arbitrary measures, since, it continued, "there
is nothing so *fretting* and *vexatious*, nothing so justly
TERRIBLE to tyrants, and their tools and abettors, as a
FREE PRESS." A banquet held to celebrate the repeal
of the Stamp Act was marked by a toast to "the *Boston
Gazette* and the Worthy Members of the House who have
vindicated the freedom of the press."[1]

It seemed to Chief Justice Hutchinson that libelling
was threatening subversion of all order, and he told the
grand jury that the freest government in Europe would
not have tolerated the freedom used in the Boston papers.
He anticipated, he said, that some people would cry out
that he was striking at the liberty of the press, but he
thought that the first magistrate in the province should
not be slandered with impunity in "infamous papers,"
and that the restraint of libels was necessary in order to
preserve liberty. "Formerly," said he, "no Man could
print his Thoughts, ever so modestly and calmly, or with
ever so much Candour and Ingenuousness, upon any Subject
whatever, without a Licence. When this Restraint was
taken off, then was the true Liberty of the Press." Not

---

[1] There were many references in the newspapers of other colonies to the
maintenance of freedom of the press. See *New Jersey Archives*, xi, xii, xix,
passim. The *Pennsylvania Journal* of September 11, 1766, contained this
passage: "To the freedom of the press in America, we may in a great measure
attribute the continuance of those inherent and constitutional privileges, which
we yet enjoy and which every Briton, who is not enslaved to private or party
interests prefers to his life. We cannot therefore doubt, but that the happi-
ness, which now reigns through all the British plantations, will inspire every
friend of his country with an honest and generous indignation against the
wretch that would attempt to enslave his countrymen by restraints on the
press" (quoted in *Magazine of History*, July, 1905, p. 65).

even this charge, however, availed to induce the grand jury to present indictments for the libel on the governor.[1]

Now that the spreading of libels was given the protection of immunity from prosecution, Hutchinson became too much discouraged to expect again that grand juries would indict libellers. He declared that he had no hope of the cessation of "this atrocious crime," except in the fact that libels multiplied so fast, became "so common, so scandalous, so entirely false and miscreditable," that everybody would treat them with neglect. Yet he joined with the commissioners of the customs resident in Boston in complaints against the "licentiousness" of the press,[2] and induced the home government to take up the matter seriously.

In 1770 a committee of the Lords of the Council for Plantation Affairs brought the indictment against Massachusetts, "that seditious and libellous publications are encouraged, and go unpunished, manifesting a design to stir up the people to acts of violence and opposition to the laws, and to the authority of Parliament." To these charges the governor's Council replied as follows through William Bollan, the agent in England : —

> As to the first, that seditious and libellous papers going unpunished, &c.; allowing that to be the case, where doth the fault lie? Not in the Council. Can they try and determine these matters? In this way, they have nothing to do with them. Why is there not a charge against the House of Lords, (which is the *summa curia*,) that they do not suppress those seditious and libellous publications at home? If we have any amongst us, there are fifty in England to one here.

[1] Quincy, *Massachusetts Reports*, 266; Hutchinson, *Massachusetts*, iii. 186; Almon, *Prior Documents*, 199–202; *House Journal*, 1768, pp. 206–211 *passim*.
[2] Bancroft, *United States* (1854), vi. 128; *Massachusetts Archives*, xxvi. 370, 372, 373.

K

> Must the English constitution, then, so far as it
> relates to the House of Lords, be altered, because
> they do not do that, which, by law, they cannot
> do; and, which, if they did, would be an infrac-
> tion of the constitutional rights of Englishmen.[1]

The Council, however, showed a willingness to comply
formally with the demand for proceedings against the
printers; for it summoned Isaiah Thomas, of the *Massachusetts Spy*, to appear and answer for publishing a political communication in his paper of November 14, 1771.
As Thomas would not obey a verbal order conveyed by
the messenger, the Council advised that the attorney-
general be directed to file an information against him, a
proposition which brought out such ardent protests from
the writers of the opposition that the action was dropped.[2]
Again, in September, 1772, the boldness of the *Spy*
attracted the special attention of the Council, which this
time also passed a futile vote advising the governor to
direct the attorney-general to prosecute the author or publisher of these "high reflections" upon the government.[3]
Probably it was not expected that the advice would be
acted upon, since it must have been apparent that the
seriousness of the political crisis could not be lessened by
threats of restraints upon the press. At any rate, the law
officers did not venture a test of strength in prosecutions
which would have been effective only in increasing popular resentment.[4]

[1] Bradford, *State Papers*, 273 ff. The significance of this retort as to English conditions will be appreciated when the contemporary struggles over
publications by Wilkes, Junius, Almon, Woodfall, and others are recalled.
See Bourne, *English Newspapers*, i. chs. vi–vii.

[2] Thomas, *History of Printing*, i. 166–168; *Council Records*, xvi. 596–597,
600.

[3] *Council Records*, xvi. 665, 666 (September 24 and October 1, 1772).

[4] Royal officials in other colonies besides Massachusetts made complaints
about freedom of discussion in the press from 1763 to 1775. Colden wrote

The last years of debate over imperial and colonial
rights were characterized by a non-legal, but very real,
invasion of rights of freedom of discussion. The radical
party became utterly intolerant of open defence of the
policy of king and Parliament by its conservative opponents.
Riotous demonstrations, boycotts, and mob violence were
directed against the authors, or supposed authors, of articles and pamphlets which were not agreeable to the
popular taste.[1] One newspaper in Boston, the *Gazette
and Post-Boy*, found the struggle for existence against
public sentiment so unprofitable that it ceased publication
in 1775, before the outbreak of war, leaving the *News-
Letter* as the sole loyalist and administration organ under
the protection of the governor. All questions of freedom
or restraint of the press became subordinate to the supreme
issue of loyalty or disloyalty to one or the other of the
contending parties. The beginning of actual hostilities
involved, as a matter of course, the suspension of ordinary
rules of law and government, the press receiving no
exemption from the arbitrary laws of war. Newspapers
and pamphlets favorable to the Revolutionary cause were
suppressed by British officers wherever their jurisdiction
extended ; and the restraint of loyalist publications was involved in the rigorous proscription of all enemies of the
new governments by the Americans wherever their armies

elaborately on the subject, confessing in one letter : " I agreed with the Gentlemen of the Council that considering the present temper of the people this is
not a proper time to prosecute the Printers and Publishers of the seditious
Papers. The Attorney General likewise told me that he does not think himself safe to commence such Prosecution " (*New York Colonial Documents*, vii.
759–760). Again he complained: " Every suggestion that could tend to
lessen the attachment to the mother Country and to raise an Odium against
her have been repeatedly published. The People are familiarized to read
seditious if not treasonable Papers. — Of these notorious Proceedings the
Courts of Justice have not taken the least notice, or made the smallest attempt
to suppress or discountenance them " (*Ibid.* 996).

[1] See Tyler, *Literary History of the American Revolution*, i, *passim.*

were in control.[1]   The publication of the *Boston Evening-
Post*, the *Boston Gazette*, and the *Massachusetts Spy* had
to be given up in Boston early in April, 1775 ; but the
Gazette and the *Spy* were able to resume their issues in
Watertown and Worcester beyond the reach of British
arms.   The *News-Letter* continued to appear in Boston
until the British were compelled to evacuate the city in
1776, when the patriot journals in turn had exclusive
rights in the capital.[2]

In Massachusetts as a state, the people did not have
their attention particularly drawn to the legal position of
the press until their proposed state constitutions were
under consideration.   The rejection of the constitution
submitted by the convention of the General Court in
1778,[3] was largely due to the omission of a bill of rights,
in which a declaration for freedom of the press might
naturally have found a place.[4]   Virginia having set the

[1] There is a growing literature on the subject of loyalists in the American
Revolution which fully illustrates this statement.   See the works of Sabine,
Ryerson, Tyler, Van Tyne, Flick.

[2] See Thomas, *History of Printing*, ii, *passim*, but especially pp. 27, 49, 55,
58, 59, 60, 65, as to the Massachusetts newspapers.   An item quoted in Force,
American Archives, 4th series, iii. 712, stated that John Gill was imprisoned
in Boston for twenty-nine days in September, 1775, " for printing sedition,
treason, and rebellion."

[3] The convention took the strictest precautions to keep its proceedings
secret during the discussions on the form of the proposed constitution.   The
people were to have only the final result for their consideration, without
having exerted any pressure of public opinion on the deliberations of their
representatives (see *Massachusetts Archives*, clvi. 210; also an unpublished
thesis in the library of Harvard University, by Dr. F. E. Haynes, on " The
Struggle for the Constitution in Massachusetts, 1774–1780," p. 90).   Nevertheless, there was some anticipatory discussion through the press (see, for
example, the *Continental Journal and Weekly Advertiser*, January 8 and 15,
1778).   The journal of the convention, which is in *Massachusetts Archives*,
clvi, shows no reference to freedom of the press, even as a possible subject
to be provided for in the new instrument of government.

[4] The lack of a bill of rights was emphasized in the statements of reasons
for the rejection of the constitution by the town-meetings of Lenox, Brook-

precedent of protecting freedom of the press by a constitutional guarantee, and this example having been followed by seven of the other new state governments, the omission of such a provision in Massachusetts ran counter to the current of the political thought of the day. The return of the Lenox town-meeting contained the following clause, which was perhaps a typical endorsement of a carefully limited freedom of the press: "We further suppose that by a Constitution the printing presses ought to be declared free for any Person who might undertake to examine the proceedings of the Legislature or any part of Government." [1]

In the new convention for forming another constitution, John Adams was the leading member of the committee appointed to draft and propose a form of government for the commonwealth; and in the report which he drew up, he reflected the undoubted opinion of the people by including an elaborate declaration of rights. The phrasing of his seventeenth article in the first part seems to have been derived from the Vermont constitution of 1777, which was copied almost literally : —

Article XVII. The people have a right to the freedom of speaking, writing, and publishing their sentiments. The liberty of the press, therefore, ought not to be restrained.[2]

line, Plymouth, Beverly, Westminster, Lexington, Dartmouth, and Stoughton (see *Massachusetts Archives*, clvi. 381, 395, 426, 432, clx. 17, 24; also see *Continental Journal and Weekly Advertiser*, June 11 and 18, 1778, a paper which had printed adverse criticisms on the constitution, including this same consideration, on April 2, 9, and 16). General " declarations of rights " or "bills of rights " had been included in eight of the eleven new state constitutions promulgated before the people of Massachusetts voted upon their proposed organic law (see Poore, *Charters and Constitutions, passim*).

[1] *Massachusetts Archives*, clvi. 381.

[2] John Adams, *Works*, iv. 227.

The proposed article, "after a large debate," was sent to a committee of three for amendments. Neither the general debate in the convention nor the discussions in the committee have been preserved; but the special committee made the scope of the article less inclusive by striking out the provision for freedom of speech and writing, and reporting a substitute, which dealt only with the press and merely stated a general political principle, without attempting any legal definition of freedom of the press. The convention accepted the work of the committee by adopting the revised paragraph as article sixteen of the completed instrument in these terms: —

> The liberty of the press is essential to the security of freedom in a State; it ought not, therefore, to be restrained in this Commonwealth.[1]

From the convention, the constitution went to the towns for ratification. Debates ensued which covered nearly every possible point in the instrument; but, among the few clauses that met with considerable opposition, the provision for freedom of the press held a not inconspicuous place. The town of Dunstable feared the spread of licentiousness by so free a press, arguing that, "there being no restraint thereon it may be made use of to the Dishoner of god by printing herasy and soforth and like wise Injurious to private Characters." Berwick, Ware, and Yarmouth agreed in recommending that the freedom of the press ought to be limited in certain cases, "where it is extended to the abuse, or injury of Private Charecters." Chelsea voted for "the following addition to said article Viz But as its freedom is not Such as to Exempt any printer or printers from being answerable for false Defamitory and abusive Publications." A number of towns,

---

[1] See *Journal of the Convention* (ed. 1832), 41. The committee had used for "is" the participial form "being," and had put "therefore" before "ought not." Otherwise its work stood as final.

including Westford, Bellingham, Stoughton, Petersham, Milton, and Boston, thought that freedom of speech should be provided for in the article, much as John Adams had drafted it. Their arguments were well expressed in the words of a committee in Milton: " For unless *this* Liberty of Speech is granted, we are apprehensive it may be dangerous in some future time, even in Publick Town meetings, to speak the truth of weak, or wicked Rulers — and thus the most regular, peaceable & effectual method of calling the servants of the People to account, & of reducing them to private life, may be in a great measure prevented." Lexington and some other towns urged the alteration of " ought not " to " shall not," because " the strongest and most definite expressions should be adopted . . . and we cannot but think that the Words — *It shall not*, are more full, expressive and definite than the Words, ' It ought not.' " A Boston committee concluded that the article should first be expanded to include freedom of speech ; then that it should be so limited as to protect freedom of discussion of public men and affairs only ; and finally that the mandatory " shall not " should be used. Following these suggestions, the voters of Boston were asked to ratify the article conditionally, if it should be amended to read thus : —

> The Liberty of Speech & of the press with respect to publick Men & their publick Conduct & publick measures, is essential to the Security of freedom in a State, & shall not therefore be restraind in this Common Wealth.

The returns from the Suffolk towns showed that the sixteenth article of the declaration of rights as it came from the convention had been approved by 982 persons, while 1132 voters preferred the alternative forms. Scattering votes in other towns made an aggregate of about 1400 unfavorable votes against an affirmative total of nearly

4000.   On June 15, 1780, it was officially announced that the people had accepted every individual article of the constitution just as it had been submitted to them; and the declaration in favor of an unrestricted but undefined freedom of the press became part of the organic law of Massachusetts.[1]

The first public debate about the practical significance of the new constitutional guarantee arose in 1785, over a state law of that year imposing a stamp tax on all newspapers and almanacs.   As in the case of the province stamp tax of 1755, there is no evidence, despite publishers' charges to the contrary, that this act was anything more than a revenue measure adopted without expectation of unfavorable influence upon the press; but the unpopularity of the very name "stamp act" gave so much effect to arguments against it that the legislature repealed the law in the following year.[2]   At the same time, however, to make good the deficiency in the state's income, an advertisement tax was levied.   Again the printers com-

---

[1] See the manuscript journal of the convention, with many interesting papers (from which these facts are drawn), in *Massachusetts Archives,* cclxxvi–cclxxvii, *passim.*   The original printed pamphlets,— (1) *Report of a Constitution . . . as agreed upon by the Committee,* (2) *An Address of the Convention to their Constituents* (on submitting the constitution), (3) *A Constitution or Frame of Government agreed upon by the Delegates,*— are in the library of Harvard University (shelf number 6347.12).

[2] A series of articles in the *Massachusetts Centinel* for April and May, 1785, are typical of the feeling against the tax.   It was denounced as "the *first Stone* in the *fabrick of Tyranny* "; if the principle of such a tax were once admitted, it might be made prohibitory by a venal House of Representatives and thus "end the liberty of the press."   It was contrary to the constitution, because it was a stab at the freedom of the press, and "whatever tends in the smallest degree to deprive the people of political information, is inimical to the principles of Republicanism."   Furthermore, it was impolitic to limit the circulation of newspapers and almanacs printed in Massachusetts, "to the ruin of a set of artisans whose exertions in the late revolution deserves a more liberal fate," while the presses of New Hampshire, Rhode Island, and Connecticut might freely send their products into the state.

plained loudly of this restriction upon their business, alleging that it was an unconstitutional hindrance to that free development of the press which was essential to general diffusion of political information. Agitation against the obnoxious tax continued until its repeal was secured in 1788, after a House committee had reported that the burden upon the printers was not compensated for by the small annual return of about £250 from the tax.[1]

The *Massachusetts Spy*, on resuming publication after a suspension of two years, enforced the lesson of the hour with a salutation of thankfulness that the paper was restored by the legislature to its constitutional liberty, and expressed the pious wish, " Heaven grant that the FREE-DOM of the PRESS, on which depends the FREEDOM of the PEOPLE, may, in the United States, be ever guarded with a watchful eye, and defended from *Shackles*, of every form and shape, until the trump of the celestial Messenger shall announce the final dissolution of all things." [2]

Enthusiasm for the security of the rights of the individual, reaching its highest point during the Revolution, had by 1784 persisted long enough to fix declarations of rights in the constitutions of all but four of the states, — Rhode Island, Connecticut, New York, and New Jersey. In Massachusetts this warmth of feeling was appreciably chilled by the disorganization of the " critical period," and especially by Shays's Rebellion. The people were convinced that some form of government must be adopted for the nation which would strengthen the union and assist in keeping the unruly elements of society in stricter subordination to law. Nevertheless, the federal constitution met with strong opposition, and was ratified by the state convention in 1788 with great difficulty. Not the least of the

---

[1] Papers relating to these taxes are found in the archives of Massachusetts, *Senate Files*, No. 718. See also Buckingham, *Reminiscences*, i. 197.

[2] Issue of April 3, 1788.

objections to the instrument as it stood was that it did not
sufficiently protect individuals from arbitrary acts of the
government, — that it would enable Congress, for example,
to stop as libellous the publication of all criticism of the
government.[1] The loyalty of the convention to democratic
principles led to a vote permitting its proceedings to be
regularly reported for the press, — the first instance of
such action by any deliberative official body in Massachusetts, and a striking proof of the revolution that had taken
place in the relations of representatives to their constituents and of the press to both the government and the
people. Furthermore, the convention passed an order
instructing the secretary to furnish an account of the proceedings to any printer who should apply for it ; but, this
arrangement not proving satisfactory, it voted to assign to
newspaper reporters positions in the hall for the taking of
minutes, a concession made in response to the following
petition : —

> To the Hon. Convention.
> The utility to the publick at large, of a faithful
> account of the proceedings, debates, &c. of the
> Hon. Convention, being taken, and published,
> being generally acknowledged — and the sub-
> scribers wishing to furnish, as far as possible,
> such an account (and being prevented, by the
> great numbers who attend in the Gallery, from
> making minutes in that place :) pray this Hon.
> Convention to allow them a place within the
> walls for that purpose. And, as in duty shall
> pray,
> Benj Russell
Adams & Nourse
> Boston, Jany 14, 1788 [2]

The strength of the Antifederalists caused the Federalists
to propose the ratification of the constitution with certain

---

[1] Harding, *Federal Constitution in Massachusetts*, 40–41.
[2] *Massachusetts Archives*, cclxxviii. 148.

recommendatory amendments covering the chief points of objection. After the scheme seemed to have been made sufficiently acceptable by private conferences and committee deliberations, Samuel Adams endangered the success of the conciliatory agreement in the convention by offering additional resolutions to prohibit Congress from infringing personal liberty, the " just liberty of the press " being the first of these rights.[1] The advocates of ratification did not disparage the importance of suitable safeguards for personal liberty, nor deprecate the protection of freedom of the press. They argued rather that such rights could never be infringed by action of Congress, since the constitution reserved to the states the regulation of their internal affairs. Neither the old federal constitution nor the one under discussion had a bill of rights, said one of them, " nor does either notice the liberty of the press, because they are already provided for by the state Constitutions, and relating only to personal rights, they could not be mentioned in a contract among sovereign states." Mr. Parsons vigorously maintained that there was not a single natural right, uncontrolled by the state legislature, that Congress could infringe; nor a single political right secured by the state constitution against the state legislature that the people would be deprived of by this constitution. " All the rights Congress can control," said he, " we have surrendered to our own legislature." The convention voted to ratify the constitution without Adams's additional recommendations, and therefore without the proposed specific mention of freedom of the press.[2] Massachusetts was content to depend for the

[1] Proceedings of the convention on February 6, 1788. See Harding, *Federal Constitution in Massachusetts*, 98.

[2] See the manuscript journal of the convention, with accompanying papers, in *Massachusetts Archives*, cclxxviii, *passim*. See also the printed *Debates and Proceedings* (1856), 178, 187, 193, 265, 347.

security of rights of free discussion upon the provisions
of her own laws.[1]

[1] Elbridge Gerry had dissented from the action of the Federal Convention
in omitting a bill of rights from the constitution.   He had particularly sec-
onded the efforts of Mr. Pinckney to insert a declaration " that the liberty of
the press should be inviolably preserved."   The decisive argument against the
proposition had been the contention that the power of Congress would not
extend to the press.   See Elliott, *Debates on the Federal Constitution*, v. 545
(September 14, 1787).

CHAPTER IX.

REACTIONARY TENDENCIES, 1789-1812, AND MODIFICATION OF THE LAW OF LIBEL, 1807-1827.

THE end of the Revolutionary period found the freedom of the press apparently fully secured in Massachusetts by constitutional guarantees.[1] The Federalist leaders of the state professed to be satisfied with the protection given by the local organic law, and resisted in Congress the proposed "bill of rights" as amendments to the national constitution.[2] Their influence prevailed in the state legislature to bring about the rejection of the first article, with its clause on freedom of the press. Nevertheless, the ratification of that article by eleven of the other states established a further prohibition of federal legislative interference with the press.[3]

The legal effect of these provisions was, however, still to be determined by the judiciary in the trial of libel cases whenever they should arise. The first of such trials in

[1] There is a suggestive contrast in the formal, affirmative freedom of the press provided for by American constitutions, and the informal, negative recognition of rights of freedom of discussion gradually accorded by English courts. See Dicey, chapter on " Freedom of Discussion," in *Law of the Constitution*. The Massachusetts newspapers, in the last years of the Revolutionary period, made frequent reference to their fortunate legal position. See, for example, the *Massachusetts Centinel*, March 24, 1784, and January 19, 1785.

[2] Elbridge Gerry, representing Massachusetts in the first Federal Congress, criticised details of proposed amendments without opposing the principle of a bill of rights. See *Annals of Congress*, i. 462-464 and *passim*.

[3] See Ames, *Proposed Amendments to the Constitution*, 185 (note), 321.

Massachusetts took place in 1791,[1] when Edmund Freeman, editor of the *Herald of Freedom*, was arraigned under
an indictment for publishing a slanderous communication
reflecting upon the private character of one John Gardiner.[2]
Attorney-General James Sullivan showed a becoming sense
of the importance of the issue before the court, which
required a discrimination between liberty and "licentiousness" of the press. He did not shrink, however, from
maintaining that the sixteenth article of the constitution
of 1780 had not altered the common-law doctrine of libel.
Quoting extensively from Blackstone,[3] he argued that the
constitutional liberty of the press consisted in putting "no
previous restraints upon publications"; that to forbid any
freeman to lay what sentiments he pleased before the
public, to subject the press to the restrictive power of a
licenser, as was formerly done, would be to destroy freedom of the press; but that to punish authors or publishers
for articles tending to a breach of the public peace by
exposure of others to public hatred, contempt, and ridicule,
was necessary for the preservation of good order. Notwithstanding the adoption of these principles by the chief
justice in his charge to the jury, a general verdict of "not
guilty" was promptly rendered.[4] The particular prosecu-

[1] Two prosecutions of earlier date were initiated in February, 1787, against
George Brock and Gideon Pond, who had published articles in sympathy with
the popular discontent of 1786. They were pardoned and their cases did not
come to trial. See *Suffolk Court Files*, Nos. 104616, 104618, 106011.

[2] The article was in the *Herald of Freedom*, February 2, 1790. A copy of
the paper is preserved in *Suffolk Court Files*, No. 105926.

[3] *Commentaries* (5th ed.), iv. 150.

[4] *Records of Supreme Judicial Court* (Mss.), 1790, p. 52, and 1791,
pp. 84–86; *Suffolk Court Files*, Nos. 105926, 106012(13). A tolerably full
report of the trial, with the indictment, testimony, and speeches, appeared in
the *Independent Chronicle*, February 24, and March 3, 10, and 17, 1791. No
controversy over the function of the jury in such a case, or over the admission
of a plea of truth as tending to justify the publication of libellous matter, is
noted in reports of the trial.

tion had failed; but a judicial construction of liberty of the press in the state had been announced, differing in no wise from the opinions of Chief Justice Hutchinson in 1768 or of the Superior Court of Judicature in 1724.[1] In effect it was affirmed that the constitutional provision of 1780 was merely declaratory of the law as it had existed for nearly sixty years, with an added prohibition of any possible reëstablishment of censorship. The effectual freedom of the press must continue to depend upon the liberality of officers of government and the independence of juries, — or in the last analysis, upon the support of public opinion.

That support was much diminished, and was even largely forfeited, by the character of the newspaper press toward the end of the eighteenth century.[2] The violence of the war spirit had encouraged a habit of intolerance toward political opponents, and vindictive denunciation of all loyalists had been supplemented by rigorous suppression of all publications unfavorable to the Revolutionary movement. Now that the establishment of peace and the organization of settled governments gave scope for the development of national parties, the vituperative powers of ardent partisans were employed against each other as domestic antagonists. Coarse personalities, vulgar ribaldry, malicious slanders, were poured forth, until it seemed to sober-minded men that unrestrained freedom of discussion was leading to the triumph of anarchy. John Adams, for example, had long been of the opinion that liberty of the press, instead of promoting the cause of liberty, might be used to hasten its destruction.[3] Becoming convinced that,

[1] Cf. chs. vii–viii, above.

[2] See B. E. Martin on "Transition Period of the American Press," in *Magazine of American History*, xvii. 273–294. Buckingham's *Reminiscences* contains extracts from newspapers of that period, illustrating their characteristics. See also Hudson, *Journalism*, chs. x, xi, xiii, xv.

[3] John Adams, *Works*, iv. 31–32.

although the regulation of the press was the most difficult and dangerous task of the statesman, its "licentiousness" must be curbed,[1] he approved of the national Sedition Act of 1798 and sanctioned its enforcement, a step in which he but represented the dominant party in Massachusetts, which gave its hearty support to this policy. Governor Sumner and the General Court endorsed the act as a necessary measure for the maintenance of the national government, and a joint resolution was passed affirming its constitutionality.[2]

In return the Antifederalists, or Republicans, of the state did not neglect to disseminate and vigorously reënforce the arguments of their party associates in Virginia and Kentucky. The Boston *Independent Chronicle* was so vehement in its denunciation of the Alien and Sedition Acts that the proprietor, Thomas Adams, was arraigned in October, 1798, in the Federal circuit court for his libellous and seditious publications.[3] Pending the trial of this case, which was continued to the following June term, an editorial in the *Chronicle* charged the members of the General Court with having violated their oaths of office when they voted, in answer to the Virginia resolutions, that they did not themselves "claim the right, nor admit the authority of any of the State Governments to decide upon the constitutionality of the acts of the Federal Government."[4] The Suffolk County grand jury promptly indicted both Thomas Adams and Abijah Adams, his clerk, for this new libel, affirming, "All which printing and publishing hath a direct and manifest tendency to stir up uneasiness, jealousy, distrust, and sedition in the same

---

[1] John Adams, *Works*, ix. 5, 13-14, x. 117; Hildreth, *United States*, v. 165 ff., 225-231.

[2] Bradford, *Massachusetts* (1835), 361.

[3] Buckingham, *Reminiscences*, i. 256-257.

[4] *Independent Chronicle*, February 18, 1799.

Commonwealth of Massachusetts, to turn the affections, good will, and allegiance of the Citizens thereof from the same, is an evil example to others, to offend in like manner, and against the peace and dignity of the same Commonwealth."

The illness of Thomas Adams prevented consideration of his case; [1] but the trial of Abijah Adams was proceeded with immediately. Once more James Sullivan, as attorney-general, was obliged to conduct a prosecution for libel. His duty now required him to advance a step beyond the position taken in the case of Freeman eight years earlier; for the offense of Adams had to be reprehended as a "public" or "seditious" libel, an attack upon an official governing body. The attorneys for the defense maintained that common-law principles of libel were inconsistent with the constitution of Massachusetts; but Justice Dana adopted the reasoning of the attorney-general, and the following verdict resulted: "The jury find that the Paper described in the Indictment is a Libel, they do not find the said Abijah guilty of printing, but they find him guilty of publishing the same in manner and form as set forth in the Indictment." Sentence was imposed by the court, requiring Adams to pay the costs of prosecution, to serve thirty days' imprisonment, and to furnish bonds in the sum of five hundred dollars as security that he would not commit the like offense during one year.[2] Thus the

[1] This illness, which proved to be fatal, also prevented trial of his case in the Federal circuit court.

[2] *Records of Supreme Judicial Court*, February, 1798–August, 1799, pp. 183–186; *Suffolk Court Files*, No. 108191(1); Buckingham, *Reminiscences*, i. 257–259. An elaborate review of the trial appeared in the *Independent Chronicle*, April 8–29, 1799. Ebenezer Rhoades, the new editor of the *Chronicle*, explained his principles to the patrons of the paper in May, 1799, as follows: "The great first principles of civil liberty are, that all legislative power proceeds from the people; — that they have a right to inquire into the official conduct of their substitutes, the rulers; — to censure public measures

previously settled ruling of the judges on the limits of liberty of the press was vindicated in practice by the verdict of a jury.

Successful prosecutions of a similar character took place in Boston in 1802 against J. S. Lillie of the *Constitutional Telegraph*, and in Ipswich in 1803 against William Carleton of the *Salem Register*. The case against Lillie again sanctioned punishment for libel upon an officer of the government in his official capacity, the injured party being Justice Dana, who had been assailed, it was charged, in terms calculated to bring him "into great hatred, contempt, and disgrace," and into danger of impeachment and prosecution for "bribery and corruption." [1] Carleton's trial was noteworthy, in that the prosecuting attorney consented, by way of indulgence, to the admission of evidence by the defense tending to prove the truth of the charges complained of as libellous.[2]

when found to be wrong, and to use constitutional means to remove those, who violate the confidence reposed in them. These principles require, that there should be a public and free examination of the doings of the government. Information on these subjects can not be generally disseminated, but through the medium of newspapers. It is, therefore, necessary to the existence of civil liberty, that these should be open to writers, who discuss freely public measures, and even censure them when faulty." See Buckingham, *Reminiscences*, i. 261.

[1] Lillie was sentenced to three months' imprisonment, and to payment of one hundred dollars' fine and costs. John Vinal was indicted as suspected author of the libel which Lillie had published, but was acquitted because of insufficient proof of the charge. See *Records of Supreme Judicial Court*, 1800–1802, pp. 228–233; *Suffolk Court Files*, February term, 1802; Buckingham, *Reminiscences*, ii. 312–314.

[2] Buckingham, *Reminiscences*, ii. 334–335. Solicitor-General Davis was the attorney who thus waived the strict rule of law. Carleton was imprisoned for two months, assessed a fine of one hundred dollars and costs, and put under bonds of eight hundred dollars to be of good behavior. Questions arising from the plea and proof of truth by the defense have been of much less importance in civil suits for libel than in criminal prosecutions, but the prevailing usage has been to admit the plea and proof of truth as a justification in private libel actions. See Kent, *Commentaries on American Law* (13th edition), ii. 32.

The application of harsh common law rules in the libel trials led to an effort in the legislature, in 1804, to secure their mitigation. The Senate took the initiative and on January 25 passed the following bill: —

AN ACT RESPECTING LIBELS.

Sect. 1st. *Be it enacted by the Senate and House of Representatives, in General Court assembled, and by the authority of the same,* that any person indicted for a Libel may give in evidence, in his defence, the truth of any matter charged in the indictment as libellous.

Sect. 2nd. *And be it further enacted,* that in any trial for a Libel, as in other cases, the Jury, under the direction of the Court, may find a general verdict deciding all questions of law and fact involved in the issue, or, if they think proper, they may find the facts in a special verdict and submit the law thereon to the decision of the Court.[1]

The measure was not passed by the House; and the rule continued to prevail that, because the truth or falsity of statements in an alleged libel was immaterial to the essence of a libel, a defendant would not be permitted to prove their truth.[2] If the fact of publication was clear, the sole

---

[1] *House Files,* No. 5536; Senate and House journals for 1804.

[2] This rule of law had been modified in several of the states before 1804. The Pennsylvania constitution of 1790 contained a new provision on the subject, which was copied later by many of the other states. It was in these terms: —

"Sec. 7. That the printing-presses shall be free to every person who undertakes to examine the proceedings of the legislature, or any branch of government, and no law shall ever be made to restrain the right thereof. The free communication of thoughts and opinions is one of the invaluable rights of man; and every citizen may freely speak, write, and print on any subject, being responsible for the abuse of that liberty. In prosecutions for the publication of papers investigating the official conduct of officers or men in a public capacity, or where the matter published is proper for public information, the truth thereof may be given in evidence; and in all indictments for libels the jury shall have a right to determine the law and the facts, under

defense must be an effort to show absence of intent to defame, together with a justifiable purpose in publishing. With respect to the function of juries, the proposed law would have been merely declaratory of Massachusetts practice, which allowed juries at discretion to render general or special verdicts, although English judges under the common law prior to 1792 had endeavored to restrict juries in libel cases to bare questions of the fact of publication.[1]

The nature of democratic government gave rise to a very difficult question regarding freedom of criticism of government officers by the electorate. Were not the people entitled to know the whole truth, whether defamatory or not, concerning public servants? And who could give this information more properly than conductors of public journals? Was it not anomalous if an editor must suffer punishment for libel upon an officer of government, when it was really for the service of the people that the truth should be made known? Was it not a "justifiable purpose and not malicious" to inform the people of facts, concerning the acts and characters of their representatives, even if those facts tended "to expose a person to public hatred, contempt or ridicule, and to provoke breaches of the peace"? And if this principle was to be adopted, did it not apply to all government officials, appointive as well as

the direction of the court, as in other cases " (Poore, *Charters and Constitutions*, 1554, and *passim*).

The national sedition act of 1798 had contained the following clause : —

"SEC. 3. *And be it further enacted and declared*, That if any person shall be prosecuted under this act, for the writing or publishing any libel aforesaid, it shall be lawful for the defendant, upon the trial of the cause, to give in evidence in his defence, the truth of the matter contained in the publication charged as a libel. And the jury who shall try the cause, shall have a right to determine the law and the fact, under the direction of the court, as in other cases " (United States, *Statutes at Large*, i. 597).

Upon the theory that the federal courts had common law jurisdiction over the press, this section was advocated as a mitigation of the law of libel.

[1] See ch. vii, above.

elective? Was it not to be extended to public comment upon all persons who were actually or supposedly candidates for office? Certainly the practice of freedom of criticism in the newspaper press in the early years of the nineteenth century was quite inconsistent with the doctrines of the common law which had not been altered by legislative acts.

Recognition of this unauthorized status was favored, in 1805, by the Massachusetts House of Representatives in its defeat of a proposal to deprive Young and Minns of the public printing. These gentlemen had published, in the *New England Palladium*, "an indecent and libellous publication against the personal character of the President of the United States," as the article was characterized by its censors. A committee reported that it was inexpedient to rescind the contract for printing made with Young and Minns, giving reasons as follows: —

> That your committee are of opinion, that the preservation of our republican constitutions, and the impartial & faithful administration of Laws enacted in conformity to them, depend alone on the knowledge, which the people may have of the conduct, integrity, & talents, of those of their fellow citizens, who have been, or who may be called to offices of trust & honor; and that such knowledge cannot be had without the free and unrestrained liberty of the press; —
>
> That our political institutions insure to every citizen the right to form opinions for himself, and to "publish truth from good motives, and for justifiable ends, although it reflect on Government, magistrates, or individuals"; — provided always that every abuse of this right be cognizable by a Judiciary tribunal, which ought, in such case, to interfere & punish.
>
> That in the opinion of your committee every citizen who may have made a publication which might be chargeable as libellous has a right to a

trial by jury; and that the law of England on the subject of libels, which holds that the greater the truth is, the greater is the libel, is not the law of this land; and that this Honorable House cannot know that to be "*indecent & libellous,*" which might be capable of proof, & which if true ought to be known.

That this Honorable House cannot try & decide upon the question of truth or falsity because it cannot exercise any Judiciary power.

That if this Honorable House should undertake to pass affirmatively upon the aforesaid motion, it would act in hostility to the provisions of the constitution; and that such act would deeply affect the freedom of the press; — and your committee believe that a precedent would be thereby established, which might lead to deplorable consequences; —

Because, by such an act public opinion might be fixed without the fair investigation essential to the development of truths, in which the community may be deeply interested;

Because, such an act might discourage individuals from announcing facts, which it might be of high importance to the public to know;

Because it might be construed into an authority in this Honorable House to censure & to punish in cases not infringing on its own privileges; — [1]

---

[1] Questions of legislative "privilege" against public discussion of acts of legislatures had been quite insignificant in the development of freedom of the press in Massachusetts. Under the colony charter, the executive, judicial, and legislative functions of the General Court were so blended that the issue of "privilege" with respect to control of the press by the government did not emerge distinctly. Separation of interests between legislatures and royal governors under the province charter tended to bring about special measures of self-protection by the House of Representatives; yet the case of Daniel Fowle in 1754 is the only one directly in point. Contests over reports of debates, such as engaged the attention of the British Parliament, did not occur in Massachusetts, probably because there were no newspaper accounts of discussions in the General Court until after the Revolution had liberalized the political system of the commonwealth.

Because it would necessarily tend to confound the Legislative and Judiciary branches of Government in the same body of men;

Because in the course of the changes & feelings incident to Governments, the practice under such a precedent might result in the worst of despotisms; that which might be exercised by an assembly convened as a Legislature.

Your committee beg leave further to report; That the only connection existing between this Honorable House and the printers of the New England Palladium by which they are distinguished from any other printers in the State arises out of a contract made by the Clerk of the Honorable Senate and the Clerk of this Honorable House with these printers to do the Commonwealth's printing for one year from the first day of July last past. And your committee are of opinion that they have performed their engagements under that contract in a manner perfectly satisfactory to their employers.[1]

However interesting this committee report was as an expression of liberal opinion, its adoption by the House had no legal effect to change the law; and the first adaptation of the law of libel to the new conditions was not to be legislative but judicial. One William Clap, convicted in 1807 for libelling an auctioneer as a liar, scoundrel, cheat, and swindler, had not been permitted by Justice Parker to prove the truth of the libel. Upon a motion for a new trial, the attorneys for the defendant argued that the Massachusetts constitution had virtually abrogated the common law doctrine of libel, and that it could not be libellous to publish truth from good motives and for justifiable ends.[2] Especially as to all public officers, — and an

---

[1] *House Files*, No. 5661 (February, 1805); *House Journal*, 1805, pp. 177, 192, 222, 235.

[2] Cf. Hamilton's plea in 3 *Johnson's Cases*, 352. The definition of principles which Hamilton advocated in that case was adopted by the New York legis-

auctioneer was then such an officer, — the institutions of "a free elective republic," ran the argument, required full admission of the right to publish truth; and the court could not, therefore, properly deny to the defense the right to prove the truth of statements charged to be libellous. The solicitor-general of the commonwealth bore testimony that he had never known a court in Massachusetts to admit a right to introduce such evidence, and then rebutted the plea by the citation of precedents in libel prosecutions of recent years based upon the authority of Blackstone. The attorney-general seemed to endorse the argument of his colleague, but declared that he should never oppose the admission of evidence tending to prove the truth of libels as to public officers, measures of government, and candidates for office. Chief Justice Parsons in his decision reiterated the familiar language of Blackstone on the nature of libels and on the inference that a libel could not be justified by proving truth; but he announced the novel dictum that publication of truth as to the characters of elective officers, or of candidates for such offices, was not libel. In the case before him, however, since the defendant had libelled an appointive officer merely, the exclusion of evidence as to truth was a sound principle.[1]

At the time of its delivery, this judicial enlargement of the freedom of the press seems to have excited no special attention, probably because the particular case was hardly more than a personal issue between Clap and the auctioneer whom he had assailed; but some three years later, when the virulence of the press reflected popular passion over probable war with England, the law of libel was again

lature in 1805 and embodied in the state constitution in 1821. Subsequently these principles were incorporated in ten other state constitutions. See Poore, *Charters and Constitutions, passim.*

[1] *Massachusetts Reports,* 4 *Tyng,* 163.

brought prominently into consideration. Justice Parker charged the grand jury of Suffolk County to investigate the lamentable licentiousness of the press, stating for its guidance the modified interpretation of the common law of libel as affirmed in the case of Commonwealth *v.* Clap.[1] This charge was followed by a number of indictments and successful prosecutions, among them one against Abijah Adams of the *Independent Chronicle* for certain reflections upon the official conduct of Chief Justice Parsons. The chief justice, disdaining the protection of his position as an appointive officer, interceded with the attorney-general to request that there should be no objection to the admission of evidence which might be offered to prove the truth of any publication against him.[2] The action of course served to emphasize the uncertainty and irrational basis of the law of libel.

Agitation over threatened prosecutions, coupled with severe newspaper criticism of judge-made law, led Governor Gerry to seek a partisan advantage from the discussion. Having obtained from the attorney-general and the solicitor-general a report upon the prevalence of libels in the Boston newspapers since June 1, 1811, the governor laid the results before the legislature in a special message on February 27, 1812. It appeared that the law officers had classified libels under two categories, — those in which the truth could, and those in which it could not, be given in evidence in justification of the party accused. They had taken no account of libels on foreign governments or distinguished foreigners, or of aspersions by editors on their brethren of the press; and yet they had noted two hundred and fifty-three libellous articles or paragraphs, two hundred and thirty-six in Federalist papers, and seven-

---

[1] Printed in the *Boston Patriot*, December 28, 1811.

[2] *Suffolk Court Files*, November term, 1811. He also joined in asking the governor to issue the pardon which Adams received after his conviction.

teen in Republican organs. For all these offenses, but ten indictments, with three convictions, had been secured against two newspapers, the grand jury having refused to return true bills on presentments against other papers. The governor lauded the principle of freedom of the press, but he recommended that its licentiousness should be checked, and that the uncertainties of the law of libel should be remedied by statute. He urged in particular that criticism of non-elective judges ought to be as free as possible. The House responded by the prompt passage of " An act declaratory of the law on the Subject of libels," which declared that in all cases of public prosecution for a libel upon a person holding office by appointment of the governor and council, the defendant might give in evidence the truth of the matter charged as libellous, " provided such matter have a tendency to show the unfitness of such individual for appointment to his office or continuance therein, any law, usage, or custom to the contrary notwith-standing." The Senate answered that the speedy approach of the end of the session did not permit the preparation of legislation to remedy the evils complained of by the governor ; but it passed a resolution sympathizing with his recommendations.[1]

[1] *Senate Files*, No. 4386, in the archives of Massachusetts, contains a series of important papers on libels, libel prosecutions, and the law of libel for the year 1811–1812. The first of these papers is a letter from Attorney-General Morton, giving Governor Gerry an account of recent judicial proceedings in the county of Suffolk on the subject of libel. The second is a petition from the convicted editor of the *Scourge*, asking to be pardoned, and admitting the righteousness of his punishment. The third is a letter from Chief Justice Parsons, desiring that Abijah Adams, of the *Chronicle*, may be pardoned. The fourth is a petition of Abijah Adams, suing for a pardon, but asserting that he had published " a fair and honest investigation of a great public question." The fifth is a petition in behalf of Adams for his pardon. The sixth is the report of the attorney-general and the solicitor-general, enumerating the libels in the various Boston papers. The seventh is the governor's special message to the General Court. See also *Massachusetts Resolves*, February 27, 1812, pp. 355–364.

In the midst of the controversy over these questions, Mr. Gerry was defeated for reëlection by Caleb Strong, and the Federalists regained control of the General Court. The new administration declared that the procedure of the late governor in investigating the publication of libels was a dangerous innovation and usurpation of the functions of courts and juries. It was even pretended that he had endangered the freedom of the press, and that the people must recur to the first principle of the constitution, "that the freedom of speech and of the press is essential to the preservation of our free governments."[1] Whatever might be said of the hypocrisy of such partisan charges, they at least offered a public guarantee that freedom of the press was not to be further impaired.

The uncertainties of the law of libel again became the subject of debate in 1820, when an effort was made in the constitutional convention to include a provision in the Declaration of Rights to the effect that, in prosecutions for libels against public men, the truth might be given in evidence and the jury might determine both the law and the fact. The chief argument against the proposal was that it was unnecessary, since it sought to establish what the law already provided for in broader terms than those of this resolution. Mr. Parker maintained that the constitution already sanctioned the doctrine that the truth might be given in evidence in prosecutions for libels against public officers, and that the jury were judges of the law and the fact under the direction of the court. Mr. Jackson even contended that, under the law as it stood, one might always publish the truth from right motives and for justifiable ends, and hence the resolution, extending only to libels against public men, would be a retrogression. Mr. Austin and Mr. Blake in vain urged that there was confusion in the law of libel, that the legislature had not

[1] *Massachusetts Resolves,* June, 1813, pp. 233–241.

altered the law since 1780, and that the constitution should make the law of libel as permanent as the general liberty of the press. No one ventured to antagonize the principle of liberal relaxation of the common law, but the convention refused to endorse the proposed declaration.[1]

Yet the libel cases in the commonwealth in the next few years revealed a lack of agreement between lawyers and publicists as to the state of the law. In 1822, Judge Josiah Quincy, of the municipal court of Boston, admitting evidence to prove the truth of an alleged libel upon a Methodist preacher, declared that the constitutional guarantee of liberty of the press authorized the publication, for justifiable ends, of facts that in the common law had been deemed libellous. This ruling by Judge Quincy led to the acquittal of the defendant, Joseph T. Buckingham, of the *New England Galaxy*, but produced public expressions of dissent from some of his fellow-lawyers.[2] A little more than a year later, counsel for the same defendant in another libel trial again offered, in the municipal court of Boston, to introduce evidence of truth. Mr. Thacher, now the presiding magistrate, reversed the novel ruling by Judge Quincy, and adhered to the precedents of Commonwealth *v.* Clap, which were soon reaffirmed on appeal of the case to the Supreme Judicial Court.[3]

The pertinacity with which lawyers for the defense contended on behalf of their clients, in the face of numer-

---

[1] See *Journal of the Convention* (1853), 538, 539–542. The general function of juries "to determine law and fact" later became the subject of considerable discussion in the convention of 1853. Among the separate propositions then submitted to the people and rejected by them, along with all the other amendments, was one specifically guaranteeing this right. See *Official Report of Debates and Proceedings*, ii. 204, 360, 503, 537, 570, 578, 701, 708.

[2] Buckingham, *Personal Memoirs*, i. 105–110. A pamphlet report of this case is in the library of Harvard University (shelf number AL 985.6.51).

[3] Commonwealth *v.* Buckingham, 1824, in Thacher, *Criminal Cases*, 51 ff.; Buckingham, *Personal Memoirs*, i. 115–120.

ous decisions, for the admission of evidence tending to prove the truth of allegations cited as libellous, was fully matched by the consistency with which the higher courts reiterated the familiar doctrines of libel. In Massachusetts, as in other American states and in the British Empire, the courts long continued to maintain practical restrictions upon freedom of the press [1] in the spirit of a system of law which recognized no affirmative right of freedom of discussion, but which sought primarily to preserve the peace and to protect the government and the reputation of the individual from injurious public criticism. [2]

As was ably said by Chief Justice Parker in his decision affirming the guilt of one Blanding as a libeller in 1825 : " The general principle decided is, that it is immaterial to the character of a libel *as a public offence*, whether the matter of it be true or false . . . because the interest of the public requires, that men not invested with authority by the laws, shall not usurp the power of public accusation, and arraign before the public, with malicious motives, their neighbours and fellow-citizens, exposing them to partial trials in forms not warranted by the constitution or laws. . . . The common law therefore is left unimpaired by the constitution, except as will hereafter be stated, and by that law, unquestionably, the propagator of written or printed tales to the essential prejudice of any one in his estate or reputation, is a public offender, and is not allowed to excuse himself by the additional wrong of proving in a court of justice, in a collateral way, the facts which he has unwarrantably promulgated." The chief justice then explained that the constitutional exceptions provided for in the application of these common law principles related to proceedings of legislative assemblies and courts, to com-

---

[1] Details of many interesting judicial opinions of this character are collected in Odgers, *On Slander and Libel* (Bigelow's edition), *passim*.

[2] See Kent, *Commentaries on American Law* (13th edition), ii. 20–34.

plaints to public bodies of the conduct of public officials, and to discussions about elective officers as allowed by the doctrines of Commonwealth *v.* Clap. He said in conclusion : " That much decried rule, that the truth is no defence in a prosecution for libel . . . is founded in common sense and common justice, . . . and indeed the code of no civilized country would repudiate it. . . . A further relaxation can scarcely take place without involving the community, families and individuals in those contentions and acrimonious conflicts which will render the social state little, if at all, better than the savage." [1]

The ill-adjustment of legal precedents with the patent facts of everyday experience in the freedom of the press was brought clearly into view by these latest decisions, and by Chief Justice Parker's remark, " If any reformation . . . is wanted, . . . none but the legislature is competent to make it." Therefore in 1827 the advocates of a more liberal policy secured the enactment of the following statute : —

[1] Commonwealth *v.* Blanding, *Massachusetts Reports,* 3 *Pickering,* 304–321. It would seem that the chief justice could hardly have been aware of the extent to which the relaxation decried by him had already been made. Perhaps he was thinking too exclusively of the old doctrine which was still maintained in England, and which was to prevail there until the passage of Lord Campbell's act in 1843 (statute 6 & 7 Victoria, c. 96). Or he may have been considering that his argument was fully endorsed by conservative constitutional stipulations in Pennsylvania, Delaware, Kentucky, Tennessee, Ohio, Indiana, Illinois, and Maine, as well as by legislation and court decisions in some other states where freedom of the press had not received constitutional definition. The contrary policy of liberality had, however, been established by the constitutions of Mississippi (1817), Connecticut (1818), Missouri (1820), and New York (1821) ; and the dire results imagined by Chief Justice Parsons under these conditions had not really been produced in these states. The policy was likewise followed before the Civil War in the new constitutions of Mississippi (1832), Missouri (1835), Texas (1836), Florida (1838), Rhode Island (1842), New Jersey (1844), Iowa (1846), New York (1846), Wisconsin (1848), California (1849), Ohio (1851), Indiana (1851), Kansas (1859). See Poore, *Charters and Constitutions, passim.*

CHAPTER CVII.

AN ACT RELATING TO PROSECUTIONS FOR LIBEL AND TO PLEADINGS IN ACTIONS FOR LIBEL AND SLANDER.

Sec. 1. *Be it enacted by the Senate and House of Representatives in General Court assembled, and by the authority of the same,* That in every prosecution for writing and publishing any libel, it shall be lawful for any defendant upon trial of the cause, to give in evidence in his defence, the truth of the matter contained in the publication charged as libellous: *Provided, always,* that such evidence shall not be a justification, unless on the trial it shall be further made satisfactorily to appear, that the matter charged as libellous was published with good motives and for justifiable ends.

Sec. 2. *Be it further enacted,* That in all actions of the case, for writing and publishing any libel, and in all actions for slander wherein the defendant or defendants may plead the general issue, and also in justification that the words written and published or spoken were true, such plea in justification shall not be held or taken as evidence that the defendant or defendants wrote and published or spoke such words or made such charge. Nor shall such plea of justification, if the defendant or defendants fail to establish it, be of itself proof of the malice of such words or charge, but the jury shall decide upon the whole case, whether such special plea was or was not made with malicious intent, any law or usage to the contrary notwithstanding.

(Approved by the Governor, March 3, 1827.)[1]

The passage of this act marked the removal of the last substantial legal restriction upon the freedom of the press

[1] *Laws of Massachusetts,* January–March, 1827, ch. 107.

in Massachusetts, so that there could be no doubt in the commonwealth in 1827 that the press was free.[1]   The protection of a just and liberal law of libel was the last sanction needed to supplement exemption from censorship and immunity from arbitrary prosecution.[2]   The common law doctrines of libel had not been abrogated by the constitution

[1] Judicial opinions continued to be marked by conservative recognition of new conditions. The act of 1827 and its reënactments in revised statutes (*Revised Statutes*, ch. 133, § 6) were interpreted as simply enlarging the grounds of defense, by giving the party indicted the option of availing himself of the plea that the matter as published was true and was published with good motives and for justifiable ends. In 1828, counsel for Child made an unsuccessful effort to establish the position that freedom of the press meant "the right to publish the truth of any person ; and to publish concerning the official conduct of an elective officer, who is a candidate for the votes of the people, whatever the publisher honestly believes, and has reasonable grounds to believe ; provided in either case, that the publication be from good motives, and for justifiable ends." Proof by the prosecution that the matter was published by the defendant and was libellous was still held to constitute a *prima facie* case, and the law would presume malice from the libellous character of the publication. The burden was on the defendant, not only to prove the truth of the matter which he had published, but also to show that it was published with good motives and for justifiable ends. See Commonwealth *v.* Child, 1828 (pamphlet report and review of the case, in library of Harvard University, shelf number 24½.111.19); Commonwealth *v.* Bacheler, 1829 (pamphlet report, in library of Harvard University, shelf number 24½.115.1); Commonwealth *v.* Snelling, 1834 (*Massachusetts Reports*, 15 *Pickering*, 321); Commonwealth *v.* Kneeland, 1838 (*Ibid.*, 20 *Pickering*, 206); Commonwealth *v.* Bonner, 1845 (*Ibid.*, 9 *Metcalf*, 410). Subsequent legislation made the burden of proof on a defendant in a criminal libel case very much less, when the law provided, after 1855, that evidence of "the truth of the matter charged as libellous . . . shall be deemed a sufficient justification, unless malicious intention is proved." See *Revised Statutes of Massachusetts*, 1855, ch. 396.

[2] The statement in the text will be seen to imply rejection of the extreme claim sometimes advanced, that freedom of the press requires utter abandonment of criminal prosecutions for libel. Nor is it necessary, in order to protect reasonable freedom of the press, that editors and authors should be protected as irresponsible agents in a system of indiscriminate publicity. Libelling is justly held to be criminal, no longer on the obsolete theory that it tends to excite breaches of the peace, but on the rational ground that it unjustifiably injures its victims. Civil suits for damages have been found to be utterly inadequate remedies for this public offense.

of Massachusetts ;[1] but these had been modified to such a degree that the rights of authors, printers, and publishers were adequately secured, though at the same time they were not released from responsibility for their acts. To be sure the printers had been accustomed for a generation to brave the terrors of an outgrown but enforceable doctrine, undeterred by occasional prosecutions and punishments; but a substantial gain for the freedom of the press could not but result when formal restraints which were practically obsolete were definitely abandoned. Slight lingering traces of intolerance in public opinion, in legislative procedure,[2] or in rulings of judges, could not hinder the natu-

[1] Attorneys for the defense continued for many years to make the futile plea that the constitution of Massachusetts had abrogated the common law of libel. See, for example, Commonwealth *v.* Whitmarsh, 1836 (Thacher, *Criminal Cases*, 441); Commonwealth *v.* Chapman, 1848 (*Massachusetts Reports*, 13 *Metcalf*, 68).

[2] In 1805 the House of Representatives had virtually renounced all claims to peculiar protection against libels, by adopting the report of the committee on the *New England Palladium* question; and in 1813 the legislature had pledged its allegiance to the principle of freedom of discussion. Several subsequent legislatures, however, dealt with violations of their privileges in public libels. The House of Representatives, in 1815, directed the solicitor-general to prosecute the printers and publishers of *The Yankee* for "a gross and indecent libel upon this legislature" (*House Files*, No. 8009). In 1823 Russell and Gardner humbly apologized to the House for having printed an offensive item (*House Files*, No. 9319). In 1824 and in 1827 special committees of the House inquired into certain newspaper items relating to its proceedings and censured the publishers, although no action against the offenders was taken (*House Files*, Nos. 9426 and 10125). The censure, in 1832, of David L. Child, while a member of the House, for a libel on the speaker, proceeded upon the theory that the House had special powers over its members for acts in any way relating to its proceedings (*House Files*, No. 11969; also a pamphlet report of the case in the library of Harvard University, shelf number 24½.11). The case is therefore hardly pertinent to the main issue of legislative "privilege" in relation to the press. Some further discussion of the question arose in 1850 and again in 1855, ending in the latter case with this judgment by a committee : "It was no part of our duty (nor had we the power, nor could the Legislature confer it upon us) to interfere with the editor or the printer. They have the right to remark upon

M

ral development of a freedom of discussion through the press which was to correspond to the social and political ideals of the people.

the Legislature, its committees, and its acts, with as much freedom and severity as they see fit to employ, accountable only to the tribunals of justice established by law, and a healthy public sentiment, often stronger than positive law. With that right we would not meddle if we could" (*House Legislative Documents,* 1855, No. 263, pp. 3-4). Formal recognition of the propriety of publishing newspaper reports of debates had been given in 1824, when the House voted "That it is expedient to admit one or more Reporters to have convenient accomodations within the Bar of the House" (*House Files,* No. 9438). Improved arrangements for the convenience of reporters were secured in 1829 and 1835 (*House Files,* Nos. 13790 and 13791).

APPENDIX A.

ILLUSTRATIVE DOCUMENTS.

Literal transcripts from original documents in *Massachusetts Archives* and *Suffolk County Records.*

I. JAMES FRANKLIN AND "THE NEW ENGLAND COURANT," 1722–1723.

1. Censure and Imprisonment of James Franklin, 1722.

In Council, the Board having had Consideration of a Paragraph in a paper Called the New Engl^{d} Courant, published on Monday last, relating to the fitting out a Ship here to proceed ags^{t} the Pyrates, & having Examin^{d} James Franklyn Printer, who Acknowledged himself the publisher thereof, & finding the Said Paragraph to be Grounded on a Letter, pretended by the Said Franklyn to be recieved from Rhode Island, Resolved, That the Said Paragraph is a High affront to this Government.

In the House of Representatives, Read & Concurred; & Resolv^{d} that the Sherriff of the County of Suffolk do forthwith Committ to the Goal in Boston the Body of James Franklyn Printer, for the Gross affront offered to this Government, in his Courant of Munday last, there to remain during this Session.

In Council; Read & Concurred; Consented to. — *General Court Records*, xi. 319–320 (June 12, 1722).

2. Proposal for Censorship Defeated, 1722.

In Council, Whereas in the Paper Called the New Engl^{d} Courant, Printed Weekly by James Franklyn, Many passages have been published boldly Reflecting upon his Majesties Government and on the administration of itt in this Province, The Ministry Churches & Colledge, and it very often Contains Paragraphs that tend to fill the Readers Minds with Vanity to the dishonour of God & Disservice of Good men, Resolved,

That no Such Weekly paper be hereafter printed or published, without the Same be first perused by the Secr^{y} (as has been Usual) and that the Said Franklyn Give Security before the Justices of the Superiour

Court, in the Sum of One hundred pounds, to be of the Good Behaviour to the End of the Next fall Sessions of this Court.

In the House of Representatives Read & Non Concurr^d. — *General Court Records*, xi. 370 (July 5, 1722).

3. APPOINTMENT OF JOINT COMMITTEE, 1723.

In Council Whereas the paper Called the New England Courant of this days date, Contains Many passages, in which the Holy Scriptures are perverted and the Civil Government, Ministers & people of this Province highly reflected on,   Ordered, That William Tailer Samuel Sewall & Penn Townsend, Esq^rs with Such as the Honb^le House of Representatives Shall Join be a Committee to Consider & Report, what is proper for this Court to do thereon

In the House of Representatives Read & Concurrd, and Mr Fulham, Mr Remington Mr Stone & Mr Knolton are Joined with them. — *General Court Records*, xi. 491 (January 14, 1722–23).

4. COMMITTEE REPORT, REQUIREMENT OF LICENSE, 1723.

The Committee appointed to Consider the paper Called the New England Courant published Monday the 14th Curr^t : are humbly of opinion,

That the Tendency of the Said paper is to Mock Religion, & bring it into Contempt, That the Holy Scriptures are therein prophanely abused, that the Revr^d and faithfull Ministers of the Gospell are Injuriously Reflected upon, his Majesties Government affronted, and the peace & Good Order of his Majesties Subjects of this Province disturbed by the Said Courant, and for prevention of the like offence, for the future, — The Committee Humbly propose that James Franklyn the Printer & publisher thereof be Strictly forbidden, by this Court to print, or publish the New England Courant, or any Pamphlet or paper of the like Nature, Except it be first Supervised, by the Secretary of this Province, And the Justices of his Majesties Sessions of the peace for the County of Suffolk, at their Next adjournm^t be directed to take Sufficient Bond of the Said Franklyn for his Good Behaviour for Twelve Months.

In Council Read & Accepted,   In the House of Representatives, Read & Concurred,   Consented to   Wm Dummer — *General Court Records*, xi. 493 (January 15, 1722–23).

5. COUNCIL ORDER FOR THE ARREST OF FRANKLIN, 1723.

Voted That it be recommended to Penn Townsend Edward Bromfield & Josiah Willard Esq^rs to issue out their Warrant for apprehending James Franklyn of Boston Printer, & that they bind him over to answer, at the next Assizes to be held for the County of Suffolk, for his high contempt of yᵉ order of the Genⁱ Assembly at their last Session referring to his Paper called the New England Courant. — *Council Records*, vii. 452–453 (January 24, 1722–23).

6. WARRANT FOR THE ARREST OF FRANKLIN, 1723.

To the Sheriff of the County of Suffolk his Undersheriff or Deputy
Greeting
You are Required in His Majesties Name to Attach the Body of James Franklyn of Boston in the County of Suffolk aforesᵈ Printer and him bring before the Court of General Sessions of the Peace now held by Adjournmᵗ at Boston for & within the sᵈ County of Suffolk In Order to his giving Bond for his good Behaviour for twelve Months time pursuant to an Order of the Great & General Court or Assembly   Hereof fail not and make return of your Doings therein unto the sᵈ Court Dated at Boston Janʳʸ 28ᵗʰ   In the Ninth Year of his Majestys Reign Annoq Dom.   1722
By Order of Court
John Ballantine Cler
[Endorsed:]
SUFFOLK: Ss: Boston: Janury: 28ᵗʰ: 1722.
By Vertue of this Warrant I made Diligent Search and I Can not find him in my precinct.   John Darrell Undersheriff.
— *Suffolk Court Files*, No. 16480.

7. RECORD OF FRANKLIN'S BOND, 1723.

Pursuant to an Order of the Great & General Court or Assembly passed at their session begun the 15ᵗʰ of November last past James Franklin of Boston Printer was Convened before the Court at this time & Ordered to Recognize to Our Lord the King In the sum of One hundred pounds with two suretys in the sum of fifty pounds each   On Condition that the sᵈ James Franklyn shall be of Good Behaviour towards His Majesty and all his Liege People for the space of Twelve Months from this time. James Franklin as Principal in the sum of One hundred pounds James Davenport of Boston Baker & Thomas Fleet of sᵈ Boston Printer as Suretys in the sum of fifty pounds each, Recognized accordingly. — *Records of General Sessions of the Peace*, 1719–1725, p. 186 (February 12, 1722–23).

8. FINAL DISCHARGE OF FRANKLIN, 1723.

Whereas James Francklyn of Boston Printer was bound by Recognisance to appear at this Court to answer to such matters and things as

should be objected against him on His Majesties behalf, more especially
for his high Contempt of an order of the Great and General Court or
Assembly; and the s^d James Francklyn now appeared; But the Bill
or present^mt Exhibited against him being returned by the Grand Jury,
with Ignoramus thereupon, the said James Francklyn was Discharged
by Proclamation from his said Recognisance. — *Records of Superior
Court of Judicature,* 1721–1725, p. 119 (May 7, 1723).

II. THE CASE OF JOHN CHECKLEY, 1724.

1. INDICTMENT.

The Jurors of Our Sovereign Lord the King upon their Oath present
John Checkley of Boston within the County of Suffolk shopkeeper for
that whereas the s^d John Checkley falsely wickedly and maliciously
imagining and Contriving his s^d Most sacred Majestys rightfull &
undoubted Title to the Kingdom & Dominion of Great Britain and
Ireland & the Territories & Plantations thereto belonging, and also the
Ministers of the Holy Gospel established by Law within this His
Majestys Province, as well as within that part of Great Britain called
Scotland, their Sacred Function and Administration of the Holy Sacraments into hatred infamy and contempt to induce & bring and to Scandalize the same, to falsify & lessen the Authority of the Holy Scriptures
& to represent even the Church of Rome as a true & Mother Church
As also to create great Jelousies Divisions and Animositys among his
Majesties Loyal Subjects of this his s^d Majesties Province, He the
s^d John Checkley at Boston afores^d on the thirteenth Day of March
1723, & at sundry other times before & after did falsely, wickedly, maliciously and seditiously publish, utter & expose to sale or Cause to be
published uttered & exposed to sale a feigned, false, wicked & Scandalous Libell entituled A Short and easy Method with the Deists wherein
the certainty of the Christian Religion is Demonstrated by infallible
proof from four Rules which are incompatible to any Imposture that
ever yet has been or can possibly be. In which s^d Libel are contained
these false feigned and Scandalous words following, Viz^t "And when
"that time shall come, as they are to most Honorable & Ancient of all
"the Nations on the Earth (Meaning the Jewes) to wit their Church
" (meaning the Jewish Church) return to be the Mother Christian Church,
"as she was at first, Rome must surrender to Jerusalem (thereby mean-
"ing & insinuating that the Church of Rome is the present Mother Chris-
"tian Church) And in another part of the s^d Libel, among other
things, are Contained these following false feigned & Scandalous words,

Viz! "With the Deists in this Cause are joyned the Quakers & other of
"Our Dissenters, who throw of the Succession of Our Priesthood. And
also in one other part of the s.ᵈ Libel there are (among other things)
the following false feigned wicked & Scandalous words, Viz! "I shall
"(meaning the Authour of the s.ᵈ Libel) say something at this time by
"way of advice to those persons (meaning the Ministers of the Gospell
"by Law in this His Majestys Province established, and the several
"Congregations under them) who madly think that there is nothing
"at all necessary to Constitute a Gospell Minister, but what they (mean-
"ing the s.ᵈ Ministers & Congregations) fondly call a good stock of
"Gifts. To these (meaning as afores.ᵈ) Mad Enthusiasts those heady
"Impostors, whose pretended Gifts are in Nothing extraordinary except
"in a furious Zeal without knowledge, & a volubility of Tongue which
"proceeds from a habit of Speaking without thinking, and an Assurance
   that is never out of Countenance for ten thousand Blunders, which
"would dash & confound any man of Sence or Modesty, or that Con-
"sidered the presence of God in which he spoke, to these men (mean-
"ing as aforesaid) I say I shall (meaning the Author) speak something
"concerning the Qualifications requisite in a Gospell Minister. And
further in one other Part of the said Libel are contained the following
false, wicked and Scandalous & malicious words, Viz! "And conse-
"quently that the Rebellion of Presbiters from under the Government
"of their Bishops is the same Case as the Rebellion (for so it is called
"Numb.ʳ 17. 10) of Korah and his Levites against Aaron. And in one
other Part of s.ᵈ Libel there are also contained the further following
false feigned & Scandalous words, Viz! "And here let our Korahites
"(meaning among others the said Ministers) of several sizes take a
"view of the heinousness of their Schism. And also in another part
of the s.ᵈ Libel are these false feigned & Scandalous words, Viz! "And
"indeed whoever would write the true History of Presbiterianism must
"begin at Rome and not at Geneva. And there is furthermore contained in the s.ᵈ Libel the following false Seditious & wicked words,
Viz! "As the necessity of Government & the General Commands in
"Scripture of Obedience to Government do require Our submission to
"the Government in being, where there is no Competition concerning
"the Titles, that is where no one Claims a better right than the Posses-
"sour (thereby subtilly by Arguments to traduce and draw into dispute
the undoubted right & Title of Our s.ᵈ Lord the King to the Kingdoms
of Great Britain & Ireland and the Territories thereunto belonging.
And also in another Part of the s.ᵈ Libel are contained the following
false and Scandalous words, Viz! "Against these we produce the vast
"Empire of Russia (which is greater in Extent than all those Popish

" Countries before named) Great Britain, Denmark, Sweden & all the
" Lutheran Churches in Germany, which will vastly outnumber both the
" Papists (and their Kinsmen) the Dissenters of all Denominations be-
" fore mentioned (meaning in the s.^d number the s.^d Ministers and Congregations as aforesaid). And in another part of the s.^d Libel are
contained the following false wicked & Scandalous words, Viz.^t " They
" (meaning among others the s.^d Ministers & Congregations as afore-
" said) imitate the Coming of Antichrist now approaching. And in the
s.^d Libel are Likewise contained the following wicked, false & Scandalous words, Viz.^t " And now let me (meaning the Author) tell our Dis-
" senters of all Denominations (thereby Meaning and including the
" s.^d Ministers & Congregations as aforesaid) that they (meaning as
" afores.^d) imitate the hardness of the Jews, who built the sepulchres
" of those Prophets whom their Fathers slew while at the same time
" they adhered to and outdid the wickedness of their Fathers in perse-
" cuting the Success.^{rs} of those Prophets. And in one other part of the
said Libel is also contained the false wicked & Scandalous words
following, Viz.^t " And if so then their (meaning the s.^d Ministers) Ordi-
" nations in opposition to Episcopacy are not only invalid but Sacra-
" lidge and Rebellion against Christ, who did institute this society and
" gave them their Charter, and if their Ordinations are null, then their
" Baptisms are so too and all their Ordinances, they are out of the visi-
" ble Church & have no right to any the promises in the Gospell. And
in the s.^d Libel or Book are furthermore contained these false wicked &
malicious words following, Viz.^t " And now I (meaning the Author)
" apply myself with a Christian Concern to our misled Dissenters (mean-
" ing among others the s.^d Ministers & their Congregations) & let them
" see & Consider that when they receive (what they call) the Sacra-
" ments of Baptism & the Lords Supper in their Congregations, they
" receive no Sacraments, Nor are their Children baptized any more than
" if a Midwife had done it, nay that it had been less guiltily done by
" her in Case of necessity than by the others (meaning the s.^d Ministers)
" in the ordinary way, whose Ministrations are not only void & null
" (if they have not a lawfull Authority) but are sacralegious, & like the
" Offerings of Korah, are Rebellion against the Lord. And in the
s.^d Libel or Book are Contained these false wicked & Scandalous words
following, Viz.^t " Let then the Common Wealths men & the Orators
" for the power of the People (if they will argue fairly and upon the
" Square with us) set down the time when Monarchy did begin in the
" World, & see if this Clue will not lead them up to the Division of
" the Nations after the Flood, which I am sure no man (Who has seen
" that account which holy Scripture gives us of it) will venture to say

"was done by the People (thereby meaning & insinuating that the Title
"of Our s^d Lord the King to the Crown was not good)   And in the
s^d Libel are contained these further wicked scandalous & seditious words
following, Viz^t. "Was there ever a time in the World when all Man-
"kind (all but the Usurpers) were all asleep.   And in the s^d Libel are
contained these following false wicked malicious & Scandalous words,
Viz^t. "The Children of Korah Dathan & Abiram were swallowed up
"with them (meaning their fathers) (which Words are a plain & mani-
"fest contradiction to the Holy Scriptures, Numbers, 26.11).   And in
the s^d Libel there are in another part these following false wicked &
feigned words, Viz^t. "Shall then the Usurpers of the Levitical Priest-
"hood be swallowed up quick into the Pitt, & is there no Judgment of
"God due to the Usurpers (meaning with others the s^d Ministers)
"upon the Christian Priesthood, was it Death for any but the Priest to
"offer the Legall Sacrifices, & may the Evangellical Sacrifice be offered
"without Offence by any hands not lawfully Ordained ? (meaning the
s^d Ministers as aforesaid).   And in the s^d Libel are contained these
further false, feigned, wicked and Scandalous words following, Viz^t.
"Can their Call (meaning the Call of the Holy Ministers of Christ
"in this Province as well as in other Places) or their Conceits (mean-
"ing as aforesaid) of any mans sufficiency enable him to take this
"Honour unto himself (meaning the Honour of a Priest)   Is this the
"Call of Aaron & of Christ ? no, but it is of Korah, and our Dissenters
"who set up upon their Gifts (meaning the Ministers & Congregations
in this Province among others).   Which s^d Book or Libel containing
the several false, malicious, wicked, Scandalous & Seditious, Expressions
afores^d.   He the s^d John Checkley on the s^d thirteenth day of March
last, and at sundry other times before And since, did publish, utter, put
up to sale and actually did sell to diverse of His Majestys loyal subjects,
to the wicked & pernicious Example of all others in the like Case err-
ing, Contrary to the Peace of Our sovereign Lord the King his Crown
and Dignity & the Laws in such Cases made and provided.   The
s^d John Checkley appeared and Pleaded Not Guilty.   Upon which the
Jury were sworne to try this Issue and after a full hearing Returned their
Verdict therein upon Oath, That is to say, That the s^d John Checkley
is Guilty.

Ordered   That the s^d. John Checkley shall pay a fine of fifty pounds
to the King, and Enter into Recognizance in the sum of One hundred
pounds with two suretys in the sum of fifty pounds each for his good
behaviour until the next sessions of this Court, and also pay Costs of
prosecution standing Committed until this sentence be performed.   The
s^d John Checkley Appealed from this Order or sentance unto the Court

of Assize and General Goal Delivery next to be holden for this County, And Entred into Recognizance himself as Principal in the sum of one hundred pounds & Gilliam Phillips Esqr & William Spikeman Baker both of Boston afores^d in the sum of fifty pounds each, On Condition that the s^d John Checkley shall make his personal appearance at the Court Appealed to, and abide the sentance of the said Court & not Depart without Licence, and that he be of good behaviour in the meantime. — *Records of General Sessions of the Peace*, 1719–1725, pp. 268–273 (July 14, 1724).

2. SENTENCE.

John Checkley of Boston within the County of Suffolk App^{lt} adsect. Domini Regis From the Order or sentence of the Court of General Sessions of the Peace held by Adjournment at Boston for the s^d County of Suffolk on Tuesday the fourteenth day of July last past, when & where the s^d John Checkley was presented by the Grand Jury for the Body of the County of Suffolk in the words following Viz. . . . [Quotes the indictment, as given above.] . . .

At which said Court of General Sessions of the Peace held at Boston as beforementioned the s^d John Checkley being found Guilty by the Jury, the Court Ordered That he should pay a fine of fifty pounds to the King, and enter into Recognisance in the sum of One hundred pounds with two Sureties in the sum of Fifty pounds each for his good behaviour until the next sessions of the s^d Court: and also pay Costs of prosecution standing Committed until the sentence be performed And now the Case after a full hearing was Committed to the Jury who were sworn according to Law to try the same, & returned their Verdict therein upon Oath that is to say thay find Specially Viz " If the Book entituled a short and easy Method with the Deists Con-" taining in it a discourse Concerning Episcopacy (Published & many " of them sold by the s^d Checkley) be a false and Scandalous Libel — " Then we find s^d Checkley Guilty of all and every part of the In-" dictm^t (Excepting that supposed to Traduce and draw into Dispute " the undoubted right and Title of our sovereign Lord King George to " the Kingdoms of Great Britain and Ireland and the Territorys thereto " belonging) — But if the s^d Book Containing a discourse Concerning " Episcopacy as afores^d be not a false & Scandalous Libel, Then we " find him not Guilty.

The Court having Maturally Advised on this special verdict are of Opinion That the s^d John Checkley is Guilty of Publishing & selling of a false & Scandalous Libel It's therefore Considered by the Court that the s^d John Checkley shall pay a Fine of Fifty pounds to the King, and enter into Recognisance in the Sum of One hundred pounds with two Sureties in the Sum of Fifty pounds each for his good behaviour for Six months ; and also pay Costs of prosecution standing Committed until this sentence be performed — The s^d John Checkley as Principal in One hundred pounds, & Gillam Phillips Esqr and George Buckeridge Marriner both of Boston afores^d as Sureties became bound before the Court in fifty pounds each accordingly. — *Records of Superior Court of Judicature,* 1721-1725, pp. 236-237 (November 3, 1724).

III. THIRD PETITION OF DANIEL FOWLE, 1754.

To His Excellency Francis Bernard, Esqr —

Captain General Governor and Commander in Chief in and over His Majestys Province of the Massachusetts Bay in New England, — To the Honorable His Majestys Council, and House of Representatives, in General Assembly convened —

The Petition of Dan! Fowle, late of Boston in the County of Suffolk, and Province of the Massachusetts Bay, now of Portsmouth, in the Province of New-Hampshire, Printer, 𝕳𝖚𝖒𝖇𝖑𝖞 𝕾𝖍𝖊𝖜𝖊𝖙𝖍, That your Petitioner was on the 29th Day of October 1754, Sent for by a Warrant to appear before the Honorable House of Representatives then Sitting, upon Suspicion of printing and publishing a Pamphlet, intitled, the 𝕸𝖔𝖓𝖘𝖙𝖊𝖗 𝖔𝖋 𝕸𝖔𝖓𝖘𝖙𝖊𝖗𝖘, and upon Suspicion only, was committed to the Common Goal in Boston, where he remained for two Days and Nights closely confined, and three Days in Custody in the Prison Keeper's House and then dismissed — And whereas it was not in the Power of your Petitioner to discover the Author or Authors of Said Pamphlet, and he was not the Printer thereof himself; which Procedure of Said House of Representatives, your Petitioner apprehends, was a grievous Hardship upon him, and is well known to be of bad Consequence to his Family, and most of the Persons who were active in that Affair, have long Since been convinced he was innocent —

Your Petitioner most humbly prays that his Case may be further taken into Consideration, that he may have Such Allowance made him, as in your wonted Wisdom and Goodness may be thought proper and adequate to his Sufferings : — All which was humbly Submitted to the General Assembly June 15th 1764; in Consequence of which, the following Order was then passed, viz —

" The Committee appointed upon the Petition of Dan! Fowle, —
" Read, and accepted, and Resolved, that the Cost recovered against
" the Petitioners on his Suit, against Thomas Hubbard, Esqr and
" others, be, and hereby is remitted to him; and that his Excellency
" the Governor, with the Advice of the Council, be desired to pay out

" of the public Treasurey the Accounts of the Gentlemen concerned
" for the House of Representatives in the said Suit — "

Which Order your Petitioner apprehends is not so fully expressed
as was intended with Respect to him, at least he is not relieved as to
the Damages he has sustained in that Affair —

Wherefore your Petitioner still most humbly prays that there may be
allowed so much as in your Wisdom shall think proper to make him
some Reparation for the Damages he has sustained

And although the honorable House of Representatives, at their
Session in June 1764, were then pleased to remit unto your Petitioner
the Cost recovered against him, on his Suit against Thomas Hubbard,
Esqr and others, yet as he never had a Trial on the Merits of his
Cause, but was debarr'd from his Action on a Supposition that the
House had the inherent Right to commit him in Manner aforesaid by
their general Warrant : the aforementioned Remittance or Release was
but a partial Relief, as his Damages Sustained by that Grievous Process were in no Part considered — And he Doubts not that your Excellency and Honors will be of Opinion that if his Action had been
Supported he should have recovered his Damages in that Suit, as his
Innocence would then have appeared and pleaded his Right : He now
humbly hopes that the Length of Time since that unfortunate Action
was commenced, may in no Ways lessen the Ardour of this Honorable
Court in redressing his Grievance, but that the Loss of Liberty may be
thought equally distressing to an innocent Individial, as to the whole
Community, and that a Breach of this Privilege, which has been the
Object of publick Complaints, may not now loose its Influence and
Energy when become the Complaint of an injured Subject, he has
Reason to expect Relief when he considers Your Excellency and Honors
known Attachment to the Sacred Privileges and Rights of the Subject ;
and he humbly hopes the Manner of your Petitioners Committment,
with all the aggravated Circumstances attending it, may become the
Serious Consideration of this honorable Court, and reflect an Honor
on your Consultations no ways inferior to that of the most august Court
of the British Nation, when a Cause of a Similar Nature was the object
of their Attention ; and after a learned and full Debate, wisely determined in Favour of the Complainants —

Your Petitioner imagines the Order of Court on the Committee's
Report in his Case, was not so fully express'd as their Honors intended,
so that he is obliged to make this other Application, and relies on the
wonted Wisdom of this Court to act on his Petition as they may judge
best, — and your Petitioner as in Duty bound, shall ever pray —

                                        Danl : Fowle

Portsmouth, New-Hampshire Octo.r 20.th 1766 —
In the House of Representatives Dec.r 8 1766
Read & Orderd that there be granted to the Pet.r the Sum of **Twenty**
pounds out of the Publick Treasury on Account of y.e Sufferings mentioned in this Petition

sent up for Concurrence

Thomas Cushing Spk.r

In Council Dec.r 9.th 1766 — Read and Concurred

In.o Cotton D. Se~cry

Consented to. —

Fra Bernard

[Endorsed]

Petition of
Dan.l Fowle
Rec.d Oct 27 1766
Com.e
Coll.o Gerrish
Maj Humphrey
Cap Brown
— *Massachusetts Archives*, lviii. 556–559.

APPENDIX B.

BIBLIOGRAPHICAL NOTES.

I. SOURCES.

1. The most important and best-known collection of original materials for Massachusetts history is that belonging to the state and deposited in the office of the secretary of the commonwealth.[1] The collection comprises numerous distinct series of records and papers. First in number and importance are the papers known as "Massachusetts Archives." This series owes its present arrangement to the work of the Reverend B. Felt, who spent the ten years from 1836 to 1846 in distributing accumulated papers by topics into two hundred and forty-one volumes. The papers range in date from 1622 to 1788, and illustrate every conceivable subject relating to the affairs of the commonwealth. Each volume has an imperfect chronological index. The series as arranged by Mr. Felt has since had two important enlargements. The first consisted of three volumes of Hutchinson Papers, restored to the state by the Massachusetts Historical Society some twenty years ago. The second was made up of eighty-two volumes of miscellaneous papers, which had been overlooked, or at least omitted, by Mr. Felt. These were repaired, classified, and bound, and were finally added to the series of "Archives" in 1896 and subsequently. The absence of adequate indexes to these great masses of papers makes the labor of an investigator very heavy. Mr. Felt's topical arrangement abounds in curious contradictions, and the same lack of judgment is shown in the volumes added in 1896. The best that can be done is to select all the volumes that seem to have any possible relation to a subject which one may be investigating, and to go through them page by page, paper by paper. There is, of course, never any certainty that some vagary in classification may not have led to the concealment of important papers in the most unlikely combinations.

[1] A detailed report "upon the condition of the records, files, papers, and documents in the Secretary's Department," was made by commissioners appointed for that purpose in 1884.

Next to the series of "Archives," the fullest use has been made of the manuscript volumes of the "Council Records," which cover the years from 1650 to the present time. Here, too, the indexes are insufficient, and the volumes must be searched page by page.

A third series, the "General Court Records," consists of sixty-eight volumes ending with 1833, the first five of which are printed as "Records of the Governor and Company of the Massachusetts Bay in New England." Although not rich in materials for the purposes of this study, the "General Court Records" were a source that could not be neglected. The Council in its executive capacity dealt with the press; and its proceedings are usually found in the "Council Records." Sometimes, however, matters that were really the acts of the Council only are found in the "General Court Records."

The archives department has various files containing papers dated since 1775. The chief collections among these are: (1) Senate Papers, from 1780; (2) Council Files, from 1784; (3) House Papers, from 1775; (4) Bills, Resolves, and Acts, from 1775.

The manuscript journals of the House before 1780 are nearly all missing; but there are over one hundred volumes since that date. The archives department has also a complete set of the printed journals since 1730.[1] The journals of the Senate, from the adoption of the state constitution, are preserved in manuscript volumes.

2. A collection of valuable papers less familiar to historical students is composed of records and files in the office of the clerk of the Supreme Judicial Court for the county of Suffolk. They comprise the following series of documents: —

(*a*) Records of the Superior Court of Judicature, 1692–1780. 34 vols.

(*b*) Minute-books of the Superior Court of Judicature, 1702–1787. 100 vols.

(*c*) Records of the Supreme Judicial Court, for the several counties, 1781–1797. 19 vols.

(*d*) Minute-books of the same court, 1781–1797. 60 vols.

(*e*) Records of the same court for Suffolk, since 1797.

(*f*) Equity Records, Suffolk, 1838 to the present.

(*g*) Probate Records, Suffolk, 1760 to the present.

(*h*) Dockets of the Supreme Judicial Court, Suffolk, 1782 to the present.

(*i*) Dockets, Equity, and Probate, 1862 to the present.

(*j*) Records of the Court of General Sessions of the Peace, 1702–1780. 10 vols.

---

[1] This set is supplemented by the volumes in the State Library, in Harvard College Library, and elsewhere. The journals were first printed in 1715.

(*k*) Minute-books of the last-named court, 1743–1773. 5 vols.

(*l*) Partitions, Executions, etc., 1716–1856. 12 vols.

(*m*) Divorce Records of the Governor and Council, 1760–1786.

(*n*) Notarial Records (of Samuel Cooper), 1795–1804. 2 vols.

(*o*) Admissions to the Bar, 1778 to the present.

(*p*) Rules of Court, 1718–1884. 5 vols.

(*q*) Early Files of Court, and Miscellaneous Papers, 1629–1800.

In 1897, the papers for the period 1629–1730 had been either almost completely restored to their original file arrangement or arranged chronologically. They comprised about 29,000 cases, which were indexed by their titles. The papers from 1730 to 1800 were in process of repair and final arrangement; but, by the kindness of Mr. Noble, the author was enabled to have search made in this later series for papers bearing on certain cases. Besides the two collections just noted, there were files "preserved in original arrangement" of many papers from 1730 to 1797.

Since 1897 the work of repair and arrangement has been going on, and about 145,000 more cases have been added to the collection. As almost every case comprises more than one paper, and some have from 150 to 200 papers, the collection is reaching enormous proportions. So far as it has been arranged, it already fills nearly 1290 large volumes.

3. The records and files in the office of the clerk of the County Court of Middlesex are very valuable for items about the early printers of Cambridge. There are no indexes, and the files are not mounted or bound, but simply preserved in boxes.

4. The files of newspapers published in Massachusetts are an indispensable storehouse of material. The collections of Harvard University, the Massachusetts Historical Society, the Boston Public Library, the American Antiquarian Society, the Lenox Library, and the New York Historical Society, are noteworthy.

5. The printed series of legislative documents, the various editions of the laws, and the reports of court decisions are most valuable sources. The collections and proceedings of historical societies (especially those of the Massachusetts Historical Society), and some local histories, print original material that is otherwise inaccessible.

II. SECONDARY AUTHORITIES.

Brief characterizations of this class of materials have been given here and there in footnotes, which will serve to indicate degrees of indebtedness to various authors ; but hitherto there has been no treatment of the particular topic under consideration which is not fragmentary and

N

incidental. The appended " List of Authorities Cited " includes titles of all the works, whether sources or secondary authorities, which give any information of special significance for this study.

III. LIST OF AUTHORITIES CITED.

ADAMS, CHARLES FRANCIS, editor. Antinomianism in the Colony of Massachusetts Bay, 1636–1638. Prince Society, *Publications.* Boston, 1894.

ADAMS, CHARLES FRANCIS. Three Episodes of Massachusetts History. 2 vols. Boston, etc., 1892.

ADAMS, JOHN. Works; with a Life of the Author, Notes, and Illustrations. Edited by Charles Francis Adams. 10 vols. Boston, 1856.

[ALMON, JOHN.] A Collection of Interesting, Authentic Papers relative to the Dispute between Great Britain and America; shewing the Causes and Progress of that Misunderstanding, from 1764 to 1775. London, 1777. — Commonly cited as " Prior Documents."

AMERICAN ANTIQUARIAN SOCIETY. Archaeologia Americana: Transactions and Collections. 7 vols. Worcester, 1820–1885.

AMERICAN ANTIQUARIAN SOCIETY. Proceedings. New series. 15 vols. Worcester, 1882–1904.

AMERICAN HISTORICAL MAGAZINE (The), and Literary Record. New Haven, 1836.

AMES, HERMAN V. The Proposed Amendments to the Constitution of the United States during the first century of its history. American Historical Association, *Annual Report,* 1896. Washington, 1897.

ANDREWS, ALEXANDER. The History of British Journalism, from the Foundation of the Newspaper Press in England to the Repeal of the Stamp Act in 1855. 2 vols. London, 1859.

ARBER, EDWARD, editor. A Transcript of the Registers of the Company of Stationers of London, 1554–1640. 5 vols. London, 1875–1894.

ARNOLD, SAMUEL GREENE. History of the State of Rhode Island and Providence Plantations, 1636–1790. 2 vols. New York, etc., 1859–1860.

BACKUS, ISAAC. A History of New England, with Particular Reference to the Denomination of Christians called Baptists. 2d edition, with notes by David Weston. 2 vols. Newton, 1871.

BARRY, JOHN STETSON. The History of Massachusetts [1492–1820]. 3 vols. Boston, 1855–1857.

BISHOP, J. LEANDER. A History of American Manufactures from 1608 to 1860. 2 vols. Philadelphia, etc., 1861–1864.

BOARD OF TRADE. Manuscript Journals in the Public Record Office at London.

BOSTON. Reports of the Record Commissioners. Boston, 1876.

BOURNE, HENRY RICHARD FOX. English Newspapers, Chapters in the History of Journalism. 2 vols. London, 1887.

BOURNE, HENRY RICHARD FOX. The Life of John Locke. 2 vols. London, 1876.

BRADFORD, ALDEN. History of Massachusetts, 1764–1820. 3 vols. Boston, 1822–1829. — Also an edition in one volume, 1620–1820, Boston, 1835.

[BRADFORD, ALDEN, editor]. Speeches of the Governors of Massachusetts, from 1765 to 1775; and the Answers of the House of Representatives to the same. Boston, 1818. — Commonly called "State Papers."

BRADFORD, WILLIAM. History of Plymouth Plantation. Edited by Charles Deane. Boston, 1856.

BUCKINGHAM, JOSEPH T. Personal Memoirs and Recollections of Editorial Life. 2 vols. Boston, 1852.

BUCKINGHAM, JOSEPH T. Specimens of Newspaper Literature, with Personal Memoirs, Anecdotes, and Reminiscences. 2 vols. Boston, 1850.

BYINGTON, EZRA HOYT. The Puritan in England and New England. Boston, 1897.

CHALMERS, GEORGE. An Introduction to the History of the Revolt of the American Colonies. 2 vols. Boston, 1845.

CHANDLER, PELEG W. American Criminal Trials. 2 vols. Boston, etc., 1841–1844.

[COBBETT, WILLIAM.] The Parliamentary History of England, from the Earliest Period to the year 1803. 36 vols. London, 1806–1820.

COLONIAL SOCIETY OF MASSACHUSETTS. Publications. Vols. i, iii, v, vi, published. Boston, 1895–1904.

DAVIS, ANDREW MCFARLAND. The Cambridge Press. American Antiquarian Society, *Proceedings*, April 25, 1888. Worcester.

DAVIS, ANDREW MCFARLAND. Transcripts (MSS.) of Harvard College Records. In Harvard College Library.

DEXTER, HENRY MARTYN. Congregationalism of the last three hundred years, as seen in its literature. New York, 1880.

DICEY, ALBERT VENN. Introduction to the Study of the Law of the Constitution. 3d edition. London, 1889.

DRAKE, SAMUEL GARDNER. The History and Antiquities of Boston, 1630–1770. Boston, 1856.

ELIOT, JOHN. A Biographical Dictionary, containing a Brief Account of the First Settlers . . . in New England. Salem, etc., 1809.

ENCYCLOPÆDIA BRITANNICA (The), a Dictionary of Arts, Sciences, and General Literature. 9th edition. 25 vols. (including index volume). Boston, 1875–1889.

ESSEX INSTITUTE. Historical Collections. 40 vols. Salem, 1859–1903.

EVANS, CHARLES. American Bibliography: a Chronological Dictionary of all Books, Pamphlets, and Periodical Publications printed in the United States of America, from the Genesis of Printing in 1639 down to and including the year 1820. Vol. i, 1639–1729; vol. ii, 1730–1750. Chicago, 1903–1904.

EVERETT, EDWARD. Orations and Speeches on Various Occasions. 3 vols. Boston, 1850–1859.

FELT, JOSEPH B. Annals of Salem. 2d edition. 2 vols. Salem, etc., 1845–1849.

FELT, JOSEPH B. The Ecclesiastical History of New England. 2 vols. Boston, 1855–1862.

GARDINER, SAMUEL RAWSON. The Constitutional Documents of the Puritan Revolution, 1628–1660. Oxford, 1889.

GRANT, JAMES. The Newspaper Press: its Origin — Progress — and Present Position. 2 vols. London, etc., 1871. — A third volume is entitled "The Metropolitan Weekly and Provincial Press" (1872).

GREENE, EVARTS BOUTELL. The Provincial Governor in the English Colonies of North America. *Harvard Historical Studies*, vii. New York, etc., 1898.

HALLAM, HENRY. The Constitutional History of England from the accession of Henry VII. to the death of George II. 5th edition. 2 vols. New York, 1893.

HARDING, SAMUEL BANNISTER. The Contest over the Ratification of the Federal Constitution in the State of Massachusetts. *Harvard Historical Studies*, ii. New York, etc., 1896.

HAZARD, EBENEZER, editor. Historical Collections; consisting of State Papers, and other Authentic Documents. 2 vols. Philadelphia, 1792–1794.

HISTORICAL MAGAZINE (The), and Notes and Queries concerning the Antiquities, History, and Biography of America. 23 vols. in 17. Boston, etc., 1857–1875.

HOUSE OF COMMONS. Journals, 1547–1835. 90 vols. London, *n.d.*

HOUSE OF LORDS. Journals, 1509–1817. 50 vols. London, *n.d.*

HOWELL, THOMAS BAYLY, compiler. A complete collection of State Trials to 1783. Continued by T. J. Howell, to 1820. Index volume by David Jardine. 34 vols. London, 1816–1828.

HUDSON, FREDERIC. Journalism in the United States, from 1690 to 1872. New York, 1873.

HUNT, FREDERICK KNIGHT. The Fourth Estate: Contributions towards a History of Newspapers and of the Liberty of the Press. 2 vols. London, 1850.

[HUTCHINSON, THOMAS.] A Collection of Original Papers relative to the History of the Colony of Massachusets-Bay. Boston, 1769.

HUTCHINSON, THOMAS. The History of Massachusetts, from the first Settlement thereof in 1628, until the year 1750. 3d edition. 2 vols. Boston, 1795.

HUTCHINSON, THOMAS. The History of the Province of Massachusetts Bay, from the year 1750 until June, 1774. London, 1828. — This is published as vol. iii. of the preceding work.

LIEBER, FRANCIS. On Civil Liberty and Self-Government. 3d edition. Edited by Theodore D. Woolsey. Philadelphia, etc., 1874.

MACAULAY, THOMAS BABINGTON. The History of England from the Accession of James the Second. 8 vols. New York, 1876.

MAGAZINE OF AMERICAN HISTORY (The), with Notes and Queries. 30 vols. (vol. xxx. incomplete). New York, etc., 1877–1893.

MAGAZINE OF HISTORY (The), with Notes and Queries. New York, Jan. 1905–pr.

MASSACHUSETTS. The Acts and Resolves, Public and Private, of the Province of the Massachusetts Bay. Edited by A. C. Goodell and others. 12 vols. Boston, 1869–1904.

MASSACHUSETTS. Archives (MSS.). In the office of the secretary of the commonwealth (see above, p. 175).

MASSACHUSETTS. The Colonial Laws of Massachusetts. Reprinted from the edition of 1660, with the supplements to 1672. Containing also the Body of Liberties of 1641. Edited by W. H. Whitmore. Boston, 1889.

MASSACHUSETTS. The Colonial Laws of Massachusetts. Reprinted from the edition of 1672, with the supplements through 1686. Edited by W. H. Whitmore. Boston, 1887.

MASSACHUSETTS. Council Records (MSS.); executive proceedings of the Council. In Archives in the office of the secretary of the commonwealth (see above, p. 176).

MASSACHUSETTS. General Court Records (MSS.); proceedings of the House of Representatives and of the Council in its legislative capacity. In Archives in the office of the secretary of the commonwealth (see above, p. 176).

MASSACHUSETTS. Journal (MSS.) of the Convention for Framing a Constitution, 1779–1780; with accompanying papers. In Archives in the office of the secretary of the commonwealth.

MASSACHUSETTS. Journal of the Convention for Framing a Constitution of Government for the State of Massachusetts Bay, 1779–1780. Boston, 1832.

MASSACHUSETTS. Journal (MSS.) of the Convention of 1788, with accompanying papers. In Archives in the office of the secretary of the commonwealth.

MASSACHUSETTS. Debates and Proceedings in the Convention of . . . 1788, . . . which finally ratified the Constitution of the United States. Boston, 1856.

MASSACHUSETTS. Journal of Debates and Proceedings in the Convention of Delegates chosen to revise the Constitution of Massachusetts, 1820–1821. Boston, 1853.

MASSACHUSETTS. Journals of the House of Representatives. Printed since 1715. Boston.

MASSACHUSETTS. Records of the Colony of New Plymouth in New England, 1620–1698. Edited by Nathaniel B. Shurtleff and David Pulsifer. 12 vols. Boston, 1855–1861.

MASSACHUSETTS. Records (MSS.) of the General Sessions of the Peace. In the office of the clerk of the Supreme Court of Judicature for the county of Suffolk (see above, p. 176).

MASSACHUSETTS. Records of the Governor and Company of the Massachusetts Bay in New England, 1628–1686. Edited by Nathaniel B. Shurtleff. 5 vols. Boston, 1853–1854.

MASSACHUSETTS. Records (MSS.) of the Superior Court of Judicature. In the office of the clerk of the Supreme Court of Judicature for the county of Suffolk (see above, p. 176).

MASSACHUSETTS. Records (MSS.) of the Supreme Court of Judicature. In the office of the clerk of the Supreme Court of Judicature for the county of Suffolk (see above, p. 176).

MASSACHUSETTS. Reports of cases argued and determined in the Supreme Judicial Court of the Commonwealth of Massachusetts, since 1804. 187 vols. Boston, 1851–1905.

MASSACHUSETTS HISTORICAL SOCIETY. Collections. 7 series (65 vols.). Boston, 1792–1905.

MASSACHUSETTS HISTORICAL SOCIETY. Proceedings, 1791–1903. 2 series (37 vols.) Boston, 1879–1903.

MASTER OF THE ROLLS. Acts of the Privy Council of England.

New series. 1542–1582, 1586–1588. Edited by J. R. Dasent. 16 vols. London, 1890–1897. — Included in the " Rolls Series."

MASTER OF THE ROLLS. Calendar of State Papers. Domestic series. 1547–1690. Various editors. 66 vols. London, 1856–1895. — Included in the " Rolls Series."

MATHER, COTTON. Magnalia Christi Americana: or, the Ecclesiastical History of New-England, 1620–1698. 2 vols. Hartford, 1820.

MAY, THOMAS ERSKINE. The Constitutional History of England since the accession of George the Third. 3d edition. New York, 1899.

MIDDLESEX COUNTY, Massachusetts. Files (MSS.) of papers of the County Court. In the office of the clerk, Cambridge.

MIDDLESEX COUNTY, Massachusetts. Records (MSS.) of the County Court. In the office of the clerk, Cambridge.

MILTON, JOHN. Areopagitica: preceded by Illustrative Documents. Edited by Edward Arber. London, 1868.

MINOT, GEORGE RICHARDS. Continuation of the History of the Province of Massachusetts Bay, from the Year 1748. 2 vols. Boston, 1798–1803.

NEAL, DANIEL. The History of New-England, containing an Impartial Account of the Civil and Ecclesiastical Affairs of the Country, to the year of our Lord 1700. 2d edition. 2 vols. London, 1747.

NEAL, DANIEL. History of the Puritans, or Protestant non-conformists. 5 vols. London, 1822.

NEW ENGLAND HISTORIC GENEALOGICAL SOCIETY. The New-England Historical and Genealogical Register. 58 vols. Boston, 1847–1904.

NEW HAMPSHIRE HISTORICAL SOCIETY. Collections. 8 vols. Concord, 1824–1866.

NEW JERSEY. Documents Relating to the Colonial History of the State of New Jersey. Edited by William A. Whitehead, and others. 19 vols. Newark, etc., 1880–1897.

NEW YORK. Documents relative to the Colonial History of the State of New-York. Edited by E. B. O'Callaghan and Berthold Fernow. 15 vols. Albany, 1853–1887. — Vols. xii–xv have different title-pages.

NEW YORK. Manuscripts. Volumes in the State Library at Albany.

NEW YORK. The Documentary History of the State of New York. Edited by E. B. O'Callaghan. 4 vols. Albany, 1849–1851.

NORTH, S. N. D. History and Present Condition of the Newspaper and Periodical Press of the United States. In United States, *Tenth Census*, viii. Washington, 1884.

PAIGE, LUCIUS ROBINSON. History of Cambridge, Massachusetts, 1630–1877. Boston, etc., 1877.

PALFREY, JOHN GORHAM. History of New England. 5 vols. Boston, 1858–1890.

PATERSON, JAMES. The Liberty of the Press, Speech, and Public Worship. London, 1880.

PEIRCE, BENJAMIN. A History of Harvard University, from its Foundation in the year 1636, to the period of the American Revolution. Cambridge, 1833.

PENNSYLVANIA. Minutes of the Provincial Council [1683–1776]. Published by the State. 10 vols. Philadelphia and Harrisburg, 1851–1852. Continued in six additional volumes as "Minutes of the Supreme Executive Council" [1776–1790], Harrisburg, 1852–1853. — Commonly cited as "Colonial Records."

PICKERING, DANBY, editor. The Statutes at Large from Magna Charta to the end of the eleventh Parliament of Great Britain, Anno 1761. 24 vols. Cambridge, 1762. Continued to 1807. 22 vols. Cambridge, 1763–1807.

PLYMOUTH COLONY. The Book of the General Laws of the Inhabitants of the Jurisdiction of New-Plimouth, collected out of the Records of the General Court, and lately Revised. Boston, 1685.

POORE, BEN: PERLEY, editor. The Federal and State Constitutions, Colonial Charters, and other Organic Laws of the United States. 2d edition. 2 vols. Washington, 1878.

PROTHERO, G. W. Select Statutes and other Constitutional Documents illustrative of the reigns of Elizabeth and James I. Oxford, 1894.

QUINCY, JOSIAH. The History of Harvard University. 2 vols. Cambridge, 1840.

QUINCY, JOSIAH. Reports of Cases argued and adjudged in the Superior Court of Judicature of the Province of Massachusetts Bay, between 1761 and 1772. Edited by Samuel Miller Quincy. Boston, 1865.

RHODE ISLAND. Records of the Colony of Rhode Island and Providence Plantations in New England, 1636–1792. Printed by order of the General Assembly. Edited by John Russell Bartlett, Secretary of State. 10 vols. Providence, 1856–1865.

RUSHWORTH, JOHN. Historical Collections, 1618–1648. 7 vols. London, 1659–1701.

RYMER, THOMAS [and SANDERSON, ROBERT], editors. Fœdera, conventiones, literae, et cujuscunque generis acta publica inter reges Angliae et alios quosvis imperatores, reges, pontifices, principes, vel communitates [etc.]. 2d edition. 20 vols. London, 1727–1735.

SAVAGE, JAMES. A Genealogical Dictionary of the First Settlers of New England. 4 vols. Boston, 1860–1862.

SCOBELL, HENRY, editor. A Collection of Acts and Ordinances of General Use, made in the Parliament begun and held at Westminster the third day of November, Anno 1640, and since, unto the Adjournment of the Parliament begun and holden the 17th of September, Anno 1656. 2 parts. London, 1657–1658.

SEWALL, SAMUEL. Diary, 1674–1729. 3 vols. Massachusetts Historical Society, *Collections*, 5th series, v–vii. Boston, 1878–1882.

SEWALL, SAMUEL. Letter-book. 2 vols. Massachusetts Historical Society, *Collections*, 6th series, i–ii. Boston, 1886–1888.

SIBLEY, JOHN LANGDON. Biographical Sketches of Graduates of Harvard University in Cambridge, Massachusetts, 1642–1689. 3 vols. Cambridge, 1873–1885.

SLAFTER, EDMUND F., editor. John Checkley; or the Evolution of Religious Tolerance in Massachusetts Bay. 2 vols. Prince Society *Publications*. Boston, 1897.

STRYPE, JOHN. Life and Acts of John Aylmer, Lord Bishop of London. New edition. Oxford, 1821.

STRYPE, JOHN. Life and Acts of Edmund Grindal, Bishop of London and Archbishop of York and Canterbury. Oxford, 1821.

STRYPE, JOHN. Annals of the Reformation in the Church of England. New edition. 4 vols. in 7 pts. Oxford, 1824.

STRYPE, JOHN. Ecclesiastical Memorials relating to Religion and the Reformation of it, and the Church of England. New edition. 3 vols. in 6 pts. Oxford, 1822.

STRYPE, JOHN. Life and Acts of Matthew Parker, Archbishop of Canterbury. 3 vols. Oxford, 1821.

STRYPE, JOHN. Life and Acts of John Whitgift, Archbishop of Canterbury. 3 vols. Oxford, 1822.

STRYPE, JOHN. Memorials of Thomas Cranmer, Archbishop of Canterbury. 2 vols, paged continuously. Oxford, 1812.

SUFFOLK COUNTY, Massachusetts. Files (MSS.) of Court Papers. In the office of the clerk of the Supreme Court of Judicature for the county of Suffolk.

THACHER, PETER OXENBRIDGE. Reports of Criminal Cases, tried in the Municipal Court of the City of Boston, before Peter Oxenbridge Thacher, Judge of that Court from 1823 to 1843. Edited by Horatio Woodman. Boston, 1845.

THOMAS, ISAIAH. The History of Printing in America; with a Biography of Printers, and an Account of Newspapers. 2d edition. 2 vols. American Antiquarian Society, *Transactions*, v–vi. Albany. 1874.

TYLER, MOSES COIT.   A History of American Literature, 1607–1765. 2 vols.   New York, 1890.

TYLER, MOSES COIT.   The Literary History of the American Revolution, 1763–1783.   2 vols.   New York, 1897.

WASHBURN, EMORY.   Sketches of the Judicial History of Massachusetts, from 1630 to the Revolution in 1775.   Boston, 1840.

WHEELWRIGHT, JOHN.   Writings, including his Fast-Day Sermon, 1637 . . . and a Memoir by Charles H. Bell.   Prince Society, *Publications*.   Boston, 1876.

WHEILDON, WILLIAM W.   Curiosities of History.   2d edition.   Boston, etc., 1880.

WHITMORE, WILLIAM H., editor.   The Andros Tracts: being a collection of Pamphlets and Official Papers issued during the period between the Overthrow of the Andros Government and the Establishment of the Second Charter of Massachusetts.   With notes and a memoir of Sir Edmund Andros.   3 vols.   Prince Society, *Publications*.   Boston, 1868–1874.

WINSOR, JUSTIN, editor.   The Memorial History of Boston, including Suffolk County, Massachusetts, 1630–1880.   4 vols.   Boston, 1882–1886.

WINSOR, JUSTIN, editor.   Narrative and Critical History of America, 8 vols.   Boston, etc., 1886–1889.

WINTHROP, JOHN.   The History of New England from 1630 to 1649; from his original manuscripts.   Edited by James Savage.   2 vols.   Boston, 1853.

INDEX.

Adams, Abijah, indicted in 1799 with Thomas Adams, of the *Independent Chronicle*, for a libel on the General Court, 144 ; trial, conviction, and sentence, 145 ; indictment and conviction in 1811 for libellous reflections in the *Independent Chronicle* on the official conduct of Chief Justice Parsons, 153.

Adams, John, freedom of discussion in the *Boston Gazette*, 123 ; praise of Edes and Gill for the boldness of the *Boston Gazette*, 124; author of draft of constitution of 1780 with clause on freedom of the press, 133 ; approval of national Sedition Act of 1798, 144.

Adams, Samuel, freedom of discussion in the *Boston Gazette*, 123 ; proposal in convention of 1788 of recommendatory amendment for "just liberty of the press," 139.

Adams, Thomas, editor of *Boston Independent Chronicle*, arraigned for violation of Sedition Act, 144 ; indicted in 1799 by Suffolk County grand jury for libel on the General Court, 144–145; prosecution prevented by death, 145.

"Advertisements," used in 1720 for political agitation, 91 and note.

Advertisement tax, 1786–1788, 136–137 ; repeal of, 137; insignificant revenue from, 137.

Agitation for relaxation of Massachusetts system of government, 1645–46, 30–31.

Alien printers, special privileges in England by act of 1483, 4 ; repeal in 1533 of act favoring, 4 note.

Allen, James, printer, examined by the Council, 80.

Allin, James, appointed licenser of the press, 1675, 58 note.

Amendment, on freedom of the press in the Federal Constitution, proposed by Samuel Adams in the 1788 convention, 139.

Amendments on freedom of the press in the constitution of 1780 proposed by various towns, 134–136.

"Amicus Patriae," political advertisements by, 91 note.

Anabaptists, persecution of, 34.

Andros, Governor, instructions in 1686 and 1688 regarding control of printing, 64–65, 65 note ; proceedings of his Council regulating printing, 65–66 ; his press regulations as a grievance, 66–67 ; overthrow of his government, 67.

Antinomian heresy, results in banishment of spirit of free inquiry, 21.

Appleton *v.* Dunster, cited on ownership and management of the press, 24 note.

Archbishop of Canterbury, powers in the system of censorship. *See* Censorship ; High Commission ; Star Chamber ordinances.

Areopagitica, Milton's argument on freedom of the press, 27–28.

Austin, Ann, Quaker, case of in 1659, 36 and note.